A Life of Joy

Obtaining Gladness
To Glorify God

Katie Hoffman

Ano Klesis Publishing
www.anoklesispublishing.com

Ano Klesis Publishing
www.anoklesispublishing.com

Katie Hoffman can be contacted through www.katiehoffman.org.

Copyright © 2006 by Katie Hoffman
Second Printing
All rights reserved.

Hoffman, Katie
A Life of Joy: Obtaining Gladness to Glorify God
ISBN 0-9788564-5-7
 1. Christian Women—Religious Life I. Title

Some stories in this book are true and they have been used with permission. Other stories in this book are based on composites of real situations, and any resemblance to people living or dead is coincidental.

Unless otherwise indicated, all Scripture quotations are from The Holy Bible, English Standard Version, copyright © 2001 by Crossway Bibles, a division of Good News Publishers. Used by permission. All rights reserved.

Scripture quotations marked (NIV) are from the Holy Bible, NEW INTERNATIONAL VERSION®. Copyright © 1973, 1978, 1984 International Bible Society. All rights reserved throughout the world. Used by permission of International Bible Society.

Scripture quotations marked (KJV) are from the Holy Bible, King James Version.

Scripture quotations marked "NKJV™" are taken from the New King James Version®. Copyright © 1982 by Thomas Nelson, Inc. Used by permission. All rights reserved.

Scripture quotations marked (RSV) are taken from the Revised Standard Version of the Bible, copyright 1952 [2nd edition, 1971] by the Division of Christian Education of the National Council of the Churches of Christ in the United States of America. Used by permission. All rights reserved.

Scripture quotations marked (ASV) are from the Holy Bible, American Standard Version.

Printed in the United States of America

To my sweet Savior Jesus, no joy is possible apart from You.

Contents

Introduction ... ix

1. The Journey ... 1
2. What a Happy Responsibility ... 9
3. Jesus, Our Forerunner to Joy ... 20
4. Killing the Joy Thief ... 31
5. Drawing Near to God ... 39
6. Will Work for Joy ... 53
7. Satisfied With Serving ... 65
8. From the Mouth ... 79
9. Training the Emotions ... 91
10. Spiritual Labor ... 106
11. Restoration ... 118
12. Beyond Our Control ... 134
13. Devoted Maintenance ... 148
14. Subtle Joy Robbing Sins ... 160
15. More Subtle Joy Robbing Sins ... 170
16. Examples of Joy ... 181

Footnotes ... 196

Acknowledgements

First, I must begin by thanking Him who is the First and the Last, the great I AM, my God forever, and the King of kings and Lord of lords. How thankful I am to God for opening wide the door for me to write this book. I could never have thought up or imagined what events God had planned for me, making it possible for me as a wife and mother to write an entire book.

Next, I'm so thankful for my husband who supported this book and read it for errors at least three times; and who always gave me a good, biblical exhortation when I needed it. Next, I'd like to thank my parents for their help and support. Finally, to each person who spent time giving me feedback, making suggestions, or doing edits—each of you is so special to me and I'm so appreciative of all you each have done.

Introduction

After I started writing, I began to notice something I had never given any thought to before: statistics about book sales. I realized there are a lot of people who like to buy "Christian" books that tickle their ears; books that make them feel their sin is okay; books that ignore Scripture in the pursuit of making people feel good. This is not that book. I know this book will not appeal to everybody, and for that I say "Praise God." My prayer is that this book would appeal to those on the narrow road, to compel them to run this race to win, and push them on toward that upward call of God in Christ Jesus (Philippians 3:14).

So to you on the narrow road, who don't want your ego coaxed but want to deny yourself more; to you who want to obey God at every cost; to you who want above all things for God to be glorified in Jesus Christ, I hope this book is refreshing water to you, that it will flood under areas where you may be weak and carry you to the Rock who is stronger than you. I hope this book will encourage you and exhort you, keeping you from being hardened in any way by the deceitfulness of sin.

My prayer is that you will fear God more when you finish this book; longing more passionately to see His face and dedicating yourself more completely to glorifying God at any cost—so that when all is said and done, you will have lived a life of joy through glorifying God so He is ultimately glorified in all things in Christ Jesus, because He alone is worthy of all glory and praise.

~1~

The Journey

And the ransomed of the LORD shall return and come to Zion with singing; everlasting joy shall be upon their heads; they shall obtain gladness and joy, and sorrow and sighing shall flee away.
Isaiah 51:11

My friend Debbie was going to arrive at my house in twenty minutes. It was a cool October morning, but inside my house, the air was warm and cozy. The sun outside was blocked by clouds, so the yellow lights in my kitchen brightened the room.

In the living room, my kids were happily playing, so I thought it was a good time to make some homemade sugar-wax for removing my leg hair. (Isn't it *fun* being a woman?) The recipe would take only a few minutes to make, and everything would be cleaned up before she arrived.

I had made the recipe before, so I was familiar with what I was doing. I put the sugar and corn syrup and lemon juice into the stainless steel pot until it boiled. After I had finished waxing, it was almost time for Debbie to arrive. I put the wax away and straightened up the kitchen.

I went into the bathroom to put out clean towel for hand drying, and as I left I looked in the mirror. I was horrified. Hanging down from the top of my scalp was a long, yellowish brown clump. I reached up to try and pull the gunk out, and remembered I'd just been using wax. It wasn't going to be coming out that easily.

I wondered how wax had ever got up in my hair when I was only waxing my legs. The answer was past finding out. Thankfully it was sugar wax and not real wax, so at least it was water soluble. The blue towel I had just hung in the bathroom was immersed in hot water. I put the dripping wet towel on my head and pushed down so the sugar would dissolve. I finally did get the wax out, but now my hair was dry on one side and sopping wet on the other. How beautiful I looked!

I walked back into the kitchen where I had made the wax and realized part of the light brown floor was sticky too. Ugh! I couldn't even see the wax, I could only feel it.

Right about that time I thought to myself, *Rejoice in the Lord always; again I will say, Rejoice* (Philippians 4:4). It was a definite opportunity for me to practice rejoicing because I really wanted to be frustrated. I needed to put things into perspective. Kneeling on the floor with a white paper towel in my hand, I longingly thought of how the day will come when I'll put off my corruptible body. One day I'll be with my Savior and my days of waxing will be over! I won't even have to worry about a messy kitchen. And how could sloppy hair compare to eternity in the presence of God?

LEARNING JOY

At age fifteen, I was diagnosed with mild depression. When the analysis came in, I was struck with surprise. There were things I would have changed about my life, but overall I considered myself to be fine. I briefly wondered, *Does this mean there are people who regularly feel happier than I do?* But, almost as quickly as that thought flashed through my mind, it left. I figured there probably weren't.

In evaluating my life, I couldn't recall a time when my emotional level had been any different. I began to think maybe I had always known some degree of depression. I couldn't imagine feeling any other way than I did at that time; I just didn't "feel" depressed.

Instead of feeling sad, my depression surfaced in other ways. I dreaded the thought of doing anything that wasn't exciting. If I didn't stay occupied I felt like I was going crazy. Feeling trapped and desperate at times, I longed for a way out of my emotional state. I wanted freedom from what felt like an emotional jail. But from what I knew about true joy and walking with God, the effort seemed too immense and the payoff of gladness, unrealistic. *Besides*, I thought, *why would I want to leave what I've grown so comfortable with?*

I didn't see any reason to pursue change. At that time in my life I couldn't even imagine what lasting contentment and happiness might be like. Even if I tried escaping from the bondage of depression, I didn't think I'd succeed. The risk was too great.

Now, I encountered joyful moments during my childhood when I felt close to God. Those "mountaintop" experiences had given me a taste of the peace found in Christ. But in the whirlwind of high school life the memories of those good times with the Lord were so distant. The concept of a continually joyful life seemed impossible.

At the age of five I prayed with my mom to accept Jesus into my heart. About a year before that, my parents had begun attending church. Once they started going, they rarely missed a Sunday service.

Because I was blessed to have God's Word ingrained into me during childhood, even in my darkest times of sin I was always aware that God was drawing me back to Himself. Growing up, I would walk with the Lord for a time, fall away, and try again. But, at the beginning of my senior year of high school I gave myself wholly to the Lord, put my hand to the plow, and determined to never look back. God in His grace kept me walking with Him from that point. He has never left me or forsaken me.

The change in my emotional state after I committed myself to the Lord was immediate. I was no longer drowning in deadness of emotion, but I still had a climb before I would reach the peaks of glorious joy. The more I sought and obeyed God, the more I abounded with gladness.

IT'S ALL ABOUT GOD

The story of increased joy from a closer walk with God, like in my own life, is also familiar to many women. When Carolyn first began going to a women's Bible study, she came sporadically. She'd sit quietly and somberly until asked to talk. But when it was her turn to share, she always had a story. Something "horrible" was always happening in her life and she was miserable because of it. As the weeks and months went on, things seemed to get better. She became committed to showing up at the study and sweetness began to flow from her mouth instead of sour complaints. The tenseness in her face was replaced with excitement over what God was doing in her life.

When the women asked her about all the "problems" in her life, she said most of the situations were the same. But because God had transformed her heart, her perspective on life had changed. Her vision was no longer blurred by the fog of her troubles. Through God's Word she had learned how to filter her life with truth. She had found the joy in God that was greater than her problems. That filter in her thoughts removed the granules of bitterness and made way for the sweet aroma of God's presence to abound.

The greatest source of rejoicing anyone can have in this life is found in the true and living God. Understanding the character and commandments of God is essential for learning what true rejoicing is.

Nothing that happens externally can affect you as greatly as internal changes. A woman who abounds in the joy of the Lord will be easier to get along with and more pleasant to be around than someone who is covered with the mud of bitterness and the mildew of resentment. She will be a shinier reflection of God to the world.

I challenge you to search the Scriptures with me to learn about how to replace harmful emotions with ones that come from having a healthy biblical perspective. Why should we push negative emotions off the cliff of our hearts and let them die on the trail behind us as we press on? Because we don't *have* to be tormented by frustration, anxiety, or depression.

There's no law forcing us to be miserable. Why, then, do we still find ourselves entertaining these negative feelings when they show up at our door? Is it possible to keep them locked out so we can have company with joy and gladness instead?

Not only do I *think* it's possible, but I know it is! We have numerous examples in Scripture of believers doing this very thing. Together we will look at those examples so we can learn how to be filled with joyful faith in every circumstance. It is my desire that as you read this book you would more deeply understand and grasp the joy that God desires for you. The rejoicing that pleases God resists depression, anxiety, fear, and frustration; but it can abide knowingly with sorrow and grief. This joy pleases God and complements everything He desires for us.

This is not a study on earthly, temporal happiness, but rather on the gladness our souls crave. It is the joy Peter describes as "joy inexpressible and full of glory" (1 Peter 1:8 KJV). The true joy found in the presence of God is beyond description, and the experience of it exceedingly surpasses the labor of the search.

Approximately 719 words in the Bible are translated in the King James Version into the words joy, happiness, gladness, joyfulness, delight, etc! This is definitely a subject that's important to God. Knowing how important joy is to our heavenly Father, I implore you to come to this book with a heart willing to receive His words and change where change is needed.

The more I've understood how happiness doesn't have to be regulated by outward events, the more I experience happiness in my life. I want us to pour ourselves into learning the biblical steps we can take to be more satisfied and content in Christ regardless of what we may or may not have externally.

Even if the river of your misery runs painfully deep, God can revive you in His presence with His pleasure. If the thought of inexpressible joy seems impossible to understand, I know God can transform your heart so it's filled with delight in Him. Believe with me that God is able to do exceedingly, abundantly, above all that we could ever ask or even think (Ephesians 3:20).

In my own life God has done beyond all I ever dreamed, and He continues to do amazing works. There is no limit to His power and He knows exactly what's happening in every detail of your life. God knows what decisions you have to make, the mistakes you may have made, and the plan He has for your life. The fact you are alive is proof that God is not finished with you and that His eye is still upon you. He can transform even the most hopeless and depressed woman into someone who radiates the joy of the Lord in its fullness.

God has changed me from a woman who couldn't even handle stillness to one who has soaked in the oceans of joy in His presence, as He has enabled me. By God's grace, I've had moments of immeasurable delight over His Word, so that all I share with you comes from the richness and truth of the Holy Bible. I've experienced the sweet freedom from hopelessness that is replaced only by His hope. God has worked in my own life and taught me the sweetness of His joy without a trace of despair.

In saying this, I must explain that I still have to challenge myself daily to continually rejoice. I'm aware that I have the capacity to fall into strong despair. Above all, I know it's God who keeps me and causes me to have joy.

When you feel discouraged, you can find comfort in knowing even the godliest of believers have experienced, and do experience, sadness, discouragement, and heaviness. Think of Paul the apostle, who wrote a large number of the books in the New Testament. He confessed in his second letter to the Corinthians that he had written his first letter to them with "much affliction and anguish of heart and with many tears" (2 Corinthians 2:4).

When Paul wrote that first letter to the church at Corinth, he had to tell them how to handle one of their members who was fornicating with his mother-in-law. In this situation, Paul's feelings of anguish and sorrow were appropriate.

Sometimes distressing feelings can be from the hand of the Lord. I don't in any way want to give the impression that those who grieve, mourn, or who at times feel sad, discouraged, and heavy in their souls are wrong in feeling those emotions. What I do want is to try to help you learn how to rejoice always, even in the midst of troubling emotions, so you can be like Paul, who described himself in 2 Corinthians 6:10 as "sorrowful, yet always rejoicing."

As you read this book I hope to give you scriptural tools to wield so you can replace your ashes with beauty, your mourning with the oil of joy, and your spirit of heaviness with a garment of praise (Isaiah 61:3).

There is much to lose by not rejoicing always. It would be a severe loss to miss out on knowing God in His joy. How can we understand the joy of Jesus (Hebrews 1:9) unless we've experienced real joy ourselves? It would be horrible to live as a Christian without understanding any degree of the intensity of the joy found in Christ.

The journey of obtaining gladness through glorifying God requires determination, patience, and death to self. There is no quick fix to understanding joyfulness personally without self-sacrifice and hard work, but I encourage you to purpose in your heart to do whatever it takes to rejoice always, despite how hard it may seem at times. If there has ever been a voyage worth pursuing, seeking God is it. There is no treasure worth more than knowing Christ Jesus our Lord. In seeking Him, true joy can be found. Knowing Him is the greatest prize that can ever be obtained.

Be ready to see great changes as we consider together through God's Word the most effective methods ever available for replacing depression, anxiety, and frustration with gladness and exuberant delight. (Notice the sales pitch. But, see, I can use it because the Bible is really that effective.) If you desire to experience life more fully and find complete satisfaction on a daily basis, journey with me up the path that leads to continual contentment, revealed to us through the Holy Bible.

~2~

What a Happy Responsibility

Rejoice in the Lord always; again I will say, Rejoice.
Philippians 4:4

*I*n examining joy, it's imperative we understand why this is even important. Is it really necessary to understand joy as Christians? Is there a consequence for not being joyful? Before we look at the ways appointed for us to obtain joy, let's first carefully contemplate what the Bible says regarding why we need to be joyful. In this chapter I want to answer the question: *Why be joyful?*

JOY IS COMMANDED

The Bible repeatedly commands and exhorts us to rejoice in the Lord. The following four verses make clear God's desire for us to be happy in Him: "Rejoice in the Lord always; again I will say, Rejoice" (Philippians 4:4). "Rejoice always" (1 Thessalonians 5:16). "Be glad in the LORD, and rejoice, O righteous, and shout for joy, all you upright in heart!" (Psalm 32:11). "Finally, my brothers, rejoice in the Lord" (Philippians 3:1).

 The word *rejoice* in all three of the above New Testament verses is in the present active imperative in the original Greek. This means the word is given as a command. We may not be under the law, but we've been commanded to rejoice! So as women seeking to be obedient to Christ, one of our aims is to be always rejoicing. If you desire to please God in all things, you must set your heart upon being constantly joyful.

You may say, "But Katie, you don't know my circumstances. You could never understand how difficult my life is, and how much suffering I've endured." And you are right, because I probably never could understand your exact circumstances. But God knows your life, and He understands. And the commandment to always rejoice is not mine, but God's. He knows your sorrow and the sufferings you've endured. And God is compassionate; He is filled with tender mercy. He wants you to rejoice in Him even in your grief because of *His goodness*. He wants you to learn to cling to Him tightly, and know His character so well, that no circumstances could destroy your hope in Him.

Second Corinthians 6:10 succinctly demonstrates how the servants of God are to have joy even when things are tough; and it's almost too simple, really, if it weren't so hard. They are to be "as sorrowful, yet always rejoicing." Even when the events of this life give us reason to sorrow, we need to continue to rejoice.

Consider how Paul describes the paradox of suffering and joy in his own life. He says: "In all our affliction, I am overflowing with joy" (2 Corinthians 7:4). What kind of inhuman feat is this? It's the one I want us to do, at the peril of losing our understanding of the hope of the gospel if we don't.

Our rejoicing must not be bound up in our circumstances; it must surpass the things of this life, the way an ocean's wave would not be stopped by me standing in its way: the wave would surpass me, because it has a greater driving force. Our gladness must have a greater driving force, bound up in knowing God and the longing to see His face, so nothing standing in joy's way can stop it.

God's goodness and kindness toward us is in contrast with anxiety and human depression, but it's compatible with suffering. This may sound shocking, but it is because of God's mercy that we are allowed to suffer on this earth. The course of our emotions will flow to some degree by life's circumstances, but the goal is to keep our emotions in line with what pleases God.

There is a biblical and right place for sorrow in life. Ecclesiastes 7:3 says, "Sorrow is better than laughter, for by sadness of face the heart is made glad." Even the most heartbreaking of circumstances can be used to purify us so that we glorify Christ more intensely.

Now, if your pain has been caused by the sin of another person, be assured that God does not cause any person to sin. If you have suffered due to devastating sins like abuse, such things were not done by God's leading or at His approval. We know this to be a very certain thing, because the Bible says in James 1:13 that God never tempts any person to sin!

However, God can turn ashes into beauty. Those who have suffered deep hurts and loss know that healing does not often happen overnight. But through trusting God and believing His Word, even without full understanding, there can be dancing where there was once mourning.

Isaiah 61:3 speaks of a prophesy that is fulfilled in Jesus, who will "grant to those who mourn in Zion—to give them a beautiful headdress instead of ashes, the oil of gladness instead of mourning, the garment of praise instead of a faint spirit; that they may be called oaks of righteousness, the planting of the LORD, *that he may be glorified*" (italics added). Wow! What is the ultimate purpose of our sorrow and our joy? That God might be glorified! It is all aimed at one purpose: the glory of God!

Sometimes rejoicing is the overflow of an abundantly satisfied heart, and sometimes it is a choice that must be made. It will not always be easy to rejoice, but by the empowering of the Holy Spirit, we must choose to rejoice in obedience to God no matter how we feel. At the times when our hearts would be tempted to sin against God with an ungodly depression or hopelessness, we must refocus our gaze upon Christ, who is seated at the right hand of the throne of God. Position your thoughts to stare continually into the promises of God and the glorious eternity that awaits you in the presence of our Lord. When your mind is focused on things above, rejoicing will be a natural overflow of your soul.

GOD TAKES JOY SERIOUSLY

In the last section, we saw that God commands joy. Now let's take a brief look at some history regarding God's people and their happiness. God has desired joy in His people from the beginning. During the first covenant, God's people we're primarily the Israelites. In the fifth book of the Law, God warned the Israelites of terrifying consequences they would experience if they weren't joyful and enthusiastic for the abundance of everything He had given them.

Deuteronomy 28:47-48 boldly tells them that because they did not serve God "with joyfulness and gladness of heart, because of the abundance of all things, therefore you shall serve your enemies whom the LORD will send against you, in hunger and thirst, in nakedness, and lacking everything. And he will put a yoke of iron on your neck until he has destroyed you." The next nine verses continue to describe horrific judgments that would be brought against them.

If God required a joyful heart from the Israelites, who were under the first covenant, how much more should we rejoice? We have been given the Holy Spirit of God to enable us to rejoice. They did not have the faithful promise of Jesus that the Holy Spirit would come to them and dwell in them continually, but we have received that promise. "Nevertheless, I tell you the truth: it is to your advantage that I go away, for if I do not go away, the Helper will not come to you. But if I go, I will send him to you" (John 16:7).

Jesus has ascended to the Father, and every true believer at this time has received the Holy Spirit, who is the third person of the Trinity. We are under the better covenant that is established upon better promises (Hebrews 8:6), in which our sins have been removed in Christ and we obtain grace to help us in time of need. The Israelites were under the law, but we are under grace (Romans 6:14). Sin had dominion over them, but by the blood of Jesus we have been freed from sin.

What was difficult for the Israelites is much easier for us. They had to strive in themselves to be obedient to God and to rejoice, but our rejoicing comes as an overflow of God's Holy Spirit in our lives. They did not yet have the promises in the New Testament like we have. For instance, the Bible promises that we can do all things through Christ who strengthens us (Philippians 4:13). I encourage you to pray earnestly that God would make you a woman who rejoices always, one who serves Him joyfully and with gladness of heart for the abundance of all things.

JOY IS A SOURCE OF STRENGTH

A third reason that being joyful is essential can be found in Nehemiah 8:10. Nehemiah conveys an interesting benefit of joy, saying, "And do not be grieved, for the joy of the LORD is your strength." Can you think of a situation when even though you should have felt tired, because of your excitement or joy you were filled with energy?

One of the first things that comes to my mind is Christmas morning when I was growing up. The joy of opening presents always outweighed any tiredness I would have felt on any other morning. At a very early hour I would awaken, and without a trace of tiredness I would pester my parents until they got up. The excitement I felt was enough to motivate me out of bed and erase my lethargy.

Christmas Eve was the same way. My family always spent Christmas Eve at my grandma's house, and our tradition was to eat dinner first and then open presents. But though the meal was one of the best I was served all year, I cared little about it. I was so enthusiastic about opening my presents that food became unimportant to me.

There are things in life we want so badly at times that we'll forgo basic needs to have them. An addiction to illegal drugs can be so strong that people trapped in dependency would rather have their drugs than food and sleep.

Sometimes people want to succeed in their jobs or their schooling so badly that they're willing to deprive themselves of sleep to achieve success in their pursuit. Others will stop regular patterns of eating, even starving themselves, with the aim of achieving a perfect body.

When people are willing to neglect their physical needs, it shows how badly they want the object of their desires. Nobody has to give those people a pep talk to forgo sleep or food. When people want something or someone desperately enough, their hunt becomes consuming. Is this how much you want God? Earthly achievements will not last beyond our parting breadths in these bodies. The relationship we pursue with God now will last throughout all eternity.

And worldly ambitions are fleeting, though some people will sacrifice their most basic requirements to obtain them. So then why is it often so hard for us to give up sleep and food in the pursuit of God?

Do you find enough pleasure in God that you barely notice when you've lost sleep to seek Him? Is your excitement over knowing God enough to strengthen you when you're physically exhausted? If a human enjoyment can be stronger than a physical necessity, how much more should the enjoyment of God be enough to strengthen us!

When our rejoicing over God becomes strong enough, that joy will be our strength. When you've learned to delight yourself in the Lord, the strength you need will become available to you through the passion that joyous desire provides. So a benefit of rejoicing in the Lord always is that the joy we have over God can fortify us when we would otherwise be weak.

JOY IS GOOD FOR OUR BODIES

An amazing truth is found in Proverbs 17:22—joy can speed up the healing of our bodies. "A joyful heart is good medicine, but a crushed spirit dries up the bones." Joy can increase physical healing, but a broken and downcast spirit will sap a person of health.

Depression does not only affect the emotions, it can also cause physical sickness. The word *spirit* in Proverbs 17:22 can mean "the seat of emotion". So when the core of a person is wounded and stricken emotionally, their strength withers away. The New Living Translation says it this way: "A cheerful heart is good medicine, but a broken spirit saps a person's strength." The symptoms of depression and anxiety can sometimes be even worse than those from viruses and illnesses. So when we rejoice in the Lord we are taking a powerful medicine, and without harmful side effects!

When our bodies are not functioning properly due to poor nutrition or lack of sleep, we may experience more of a struggle against our flesh to rejoice. So I encourage you, as much as possible, to get the amount of sleep you need and to eat foods that will strengthen your body. Enjoy the freedom we have been given in Psalm 127:2 to get enough sleep: "It is in vain that you rise up early and go late to rest, eating the bread of anxious toil; for he gives to his beloved sleep."

Sleep is a gift from God, so do not stay up late unnecessarily. I find I have a much harder time being motivated when I'm sleep deprived. Don't oversleep as the sluggard, and don't deprive yourself of sleep to eat the bread of sorrows. As you lie down to rest, rejoice that God gives His beloved sleep, and when you awake, rejoice again.

In addition to healthy eating, sleep, and exercise—your body needs *joy* to maintain its health. The medical field has acknowledged this fact. Studies have shown those who laugh[1] and enjoy life[2] are healthier. And I've found that being glad and at peace makes falling asleep easier. If you're angry, anxious, nervous, or worried, or if you're holding bitterness or guilt in your heart, falling asleep can be much harder.

Say you can't sleep because of money problems. The solution is simple: If you're in bed and there's nothing you can do about your finances, then *stop thinking about them*. If the financial problems are your fault and you've been unwise or sinned in some way, confess this to the Lord and think about what you'll do differently next time and then move on. Once you've confessed your sin, you *must* believe God forgives you. And if God has forgiven you, it doesn't matter who else hasn't. (Of course, if you've sinned *against* another person, seek that person's forgiveness.)

But don't continue to feel guilty after you've been forgiven by God. Don't punish yourself with feelings of guilt. Jesus took your place on the cross and it's *okay* to accept God's forgiveness because of it. In fact, it's eternally necessary for you to believe the righteousness of Jesus has been given to you by God. You'll never experience liberating joy if you're strapped down by the chains of guilt.

At night, when you lie on your bed, rejoice and meditate on how truly cleansed of sin you've been in Jesus Christ. Be glad that you don't have to work off the debt of your sins. Guiltlessness is great medicine, and can be prescribed for good sleep and great joy.

If you're angry or bitter, those sores will fester until you decide to let your anger and bitterness go. Bitterness is like bacteria in a wound. Kill the bitterness so the wounds can heal. Do this by recalling what great sins God has forgiven you of. Then deliberately decide to forgive the person who's offended you, pray for them, and then again, *stop mulling over what happened.* Let it go.

After you've cleared your conscience and chosen to still your thoughts, begin to praise God, and don't let anything else creep into your mind. Think of the great things He's done for you. Give God thanks and tell Him *why* you're thankful. Sometimes I pray things like, "Thank You so much Father that I drove to the store safely. Thank You for protecting me. Thank You that I didn't get a flat tire. My whole day would have been thrown off and I wouldn't have to been able to get as much done, so thank You Lord God for giving me that uneventful drive."

Acknowledge the little things God does for you. Thank God when you don't get a flat tire or the stomach flu. Be grateful and rejoice for what you do have, and procure the added benefit of better health through a cheerful heart.

Exercising yourself in the habit of continual rejoicing will produce more than just a benefit to your physical body internally; there will be an external benefit as well. According to Proverbs 15:13, another physical result of a joyful heart is a cheerful countenance, which is a smiling face: "A glad heart makes a cheerful face, but by sorrow of heart the spirit is crushed." You can beautify your face by way of inner joy radiating through your smile. A joyful Christian will reflect happiness in her face by a cheerful expression.

Now please know I'm not saying a woman should have a continual plastic smile on her face, because there will be times of loss and grief when it's healthy and right to mourn. When your heart is hurting, pour it out before the Lord. Don't try to hide your grief from the Lord, because He already knows, and He longs to comfort you.

Paul the apostle blessed God because of His great comfort toward us in our sadness, saying, "Blessed be the God and Father of our Lord Jesus Christ, the Father of mercies and God of all comfort, who comforts us in all our affliction, so that we may be able to comfort those who are in any affliction, with the comfort with which we ourselves are comforted by God" (2 Corinthians 1:3-4).

It's appropriate at times to weep and grieve. In those times we must seek comfort in the Lord and believe He will faithfully reassure us. But even in sorrow, God's consolation can be a cause of joy. If we're unwilling to pour out our hearts before the Lord, we can't expect to learn what it means to be "sorrowful, yet always rejoicing" (2 Corinthians 6:10).

We must run to God as our refuge in trials. When your heart is aching, even your desire to do necessary things can fade away. A broken spirit can drain a woman of her motivation. Be armed and ready with Scripture to encourage yourself in the Lord when times of defeat and sadness come unexpectedly.

When David was sad because of his enemies, he said to himself, "By day the LORD commands his steadfast love, and at night his song is with me, a prayer to the God of my life" (Psalm 42:8). He encouraged himself by remembering God's kindness to him. Be encouraged also by the kindness of the Lord God, knowing that He daily pours His steadfast love upon us.

Now let me also add, it's right and biblical to weep when others are weeping (Romans 12:15). It would be heartless to show no grief for those who are mourning. A smiling face is appropriate when others are rejoicing, but tears are right when others are weeping.

JOY IS GOD'S STANDARD FOR EVERY CHRISTIAN

A fifth reason we need to be joyful is given in 1 Peter 1:8. In this verse, Peter sets a standard for Christians to meet and explains what the experience of each Christian should be, saying, "Though you have not seen him, you love him. Though you do not now see him, you believe in him and rejoice with joy that is inexpressible and filled with glory." Does this describe you? With this verse, Peter sets forth a high expectation for Christians.

Because of our faith in Christ, it is appropriate for us to rejoice with indescribable joy. This joy is glorious and wonderful, and never fades away. It's permanent and enduring, beyond the expression of human words. Because the greatness of God is beyond our description, the joy we experience in Him is also beyond description. The zenith of inexpressible, glorified joy cannot be reached until what we want above all else is for God to be glorified.

This joy is birthed in our expectation of seeing Christ and spending eternity with him. Paul gives us a glimpse of this mystery in 1 Corinthians 2:7-10:

> But we impart a secret and hidden wisdom of God, which God decreed before the ages for our glory. None of the rulers of this age understood this, for if they had, they would not have crucified the Lord of glory. But, as it is written, "What no eye has seen, nor ear heard, nor the heart of man imagined, what God has prepared for those who love him"— these things God has revealed to us through the Spirit. For the Spirit searches everything, even the depths of God.

We have a glorious future awaiting us. Even though we have not seen Jesus, we rejoice in Him, because God has revealed in part what awaits us through His Spirit. We can begin to understand the joy of heaven in this life, although it will be accompanied by sorrow.

Why shouldn't a woman who will soon have glory revealed in her (Romans 8:18), dwell in the glorious paradise of God (Revelation 2:7), and look upon Christ's own glory not be filled with continual, indescribable joy? Glorious things await us. But we must choose to rejoice in these things by faith. Faith is the key to continual rejoicing.

Have you personally have experienced "joy inexpressible and full of glory" (1 Peter 1:8)? If not, what do you think is the reason? If you've had other times in your life when you've felt joyful or happy, consider what the difference is. I believe God empowers us to experience gladness to the fullest (Acts 2:28), but we must receive that empowering by faith. We must give ourselves wholeheartedly to rejoicing.

Sometimes we must choose to rejoice despite the state of our emotions. This is the difference between being joyful occasionally and experiencing joy on a continual basis. This joy is found in Christ alone, and without being knit to Him as your Lord, any joy you experience cannot compare to joy so glorious it cannot be described. This leads to our third chapter, our relationship with God as the foundation and root of all our happiness.

~3~

Jesus, Our Forerunner to Joy

For the LORD takes pleasure in his people; he adorns the humble with salvation. Let the godly exult in glory; let them sing for joy on their beds.

Acts 2:28

Setting out to study joy, we must lay the groundwork establishing the source of joy, which is the cross of Jesus Christ. I feel like I cannot stress the importance of this enough. The crucifixion and resurrection of Jesus is the foundation of this book. This book would be like a tree without roots if I did not cover this subject. The death and resurrection of Jesus is the gunpowder in our cannon of joy. The ball of our joyful passion for Christ would be lifeless without a thorough review of the salvation wrought for us by Jesus to propel us forward.

Now I hear some of you thinking (which is a really spectacular feat, since I'm not omniscient) that you already know everything I am going to say. You might, and really I hope you do. Fortunately, the gospel of Jesus Christ just happens to be the most life-giving subject in the world, so reviewing it that we might delight ourselves in it is like, in a very incomparable way, eating chocolate.

If you like chocolate, then you've certainly tried it before, but it shouldn't become less enjoyable because you've already had it. Whatever it is that we really love, be it savoring a particular food, reading a cherished verse in the Bible, or taking an exhilarating bike ride, we'll most likely enjoy it again and again. In the same way, we should love the gospel so much that contemplating it means savoring it.

Grasping every aspect of the gospel of Jesus Christ with all our understanding is worth the trek through possibly familiar stomping grounds. Or maybe you're really not sure exactly what the gospel is. According to a survey of sixty Christians at a Christian conference, only one person could actually explain the whole *gospel*, also known as the *good news* of Jesus Christ.[1] We must understand the gospel thoroughly to grasp inexpressible joy. In this chapter we will examine in greater depth what the good news of Jesus is all about.

It is because of the death of Jesus Christ on a cross that we now have access to God. God is the true source of all gladness and delight, and without access to Him any happiness we have will be empty and fleeting. I'd like to share Erica's story with you. My prayer is that through this story you will see how the gospel can be a boulder in the midst of quicksand for your emotions to rest on.

JESUS WAS NOT SPARED

Walking out with poise, Erica wished she could instead scream. "He'll never understand what I'm trying to say!" she thought. Even her blood felt like it was being pumped to every limb of her body by rage, and not by an emotionless physical organ.

She opened the door of her car, hoping nobody in the parking lot would notice her. She wasn't in the mood to be friendly. With one glare back toward her husband's office, she stepped into the hot, stuffy vehicle and thought of the ways she could *show* her husband how wrong he was.

"Maybe if I served him with some divorce papers," she schemed, "then he'd see what a jerk he is!" Her heart stampeded with desire to break through the brick wall of her husband's mind.

"Why is he being so selfish? I've *never* heard of any husband not letting his wife help out in her daughter's classroom. He is being so irrational. I can't stand it! What I do in our daughter's classroom during the daytime doesn't even affect him!" With her frustration cooling into droplets of sadness, she sat back in the seat and drove home emptily.

She knew her husband was being unreasonable—that he was wrong and couldn't even see it. And she knew there was nothing she could effectively do about it. Only her Lord could change her husband's heart. Defeatedly, Erica cried to the One who could help. "Please Father, cause my husband to change his mind. How can I love and reverence and submit to a man who is *so* wrong? Please show Yourself strong on my behalf."

Then, as clear as the day the words came to her, words that answered her plea. "What then shall we say to these things? If God is for us, who can be against us? He who did not spare his own Son but gave him up for us all, how will he not also with him graciously give us all things?" (Romans 8:32). She thought of how gracious her God was in giving up His only begotten Son for her. She knew the heartbreak her Savior Jesus endured on the cross. She remembered that God was still on her side even if the circumstances weren't. Even if what she wanted wasn't what God had planned for her, she knew what God had was better.

"Yes Lord, I know trials are a part of this life. But do I have to go through such unreasonable trials?" she continued in prayer. She already knew the answer. Even if the trials made no sense, and neither God nor her husband had given her any sufficient reason *why* she couldn't volunteer in her daughter's classroom; and even if none of her questions regarding her heartbreak we're answered—she realized how blessed she was that she had the cross.

She had Jesus. And knowing she had Jesus was better that any decision her husband could make. She decided to answer her previous question. "How can I love my husband?" she thought, "because I have Jesus. Because I've been saved from eternal punishment. Because nothing can ever separate me from the love of Christ. Because even if I never know why I'm being forbidden from this thing I want so bad, I know God is working it together for my good. Because of these things, I can both love my husband and trust in the Lord."

Because she recognized how much it meant that Jesus died on the cross for her, Erica was able to be sweet to her husband that night when he came home. She apologized for her disrespect toward him without even mentioning the things he'd done wrong. She continued to plead with the Lord to change her husband's heart, but she knew that even if her husband never changed his mind, God in His love for her had a reason for allowing it, and she had to trust Him. If Jesus had not been spared from the cross, and His death brought salvation for every believer for all eternity, she knew that even if she weren't spared from her trial, God would work it for good beyond what she might ever understand in this life.

THE JOY OF ESCAPING WRATH

Erica was in a difficult situation. She had to suffer with her husband even when it meant heartbreak. Like Erica, we have likely suffered because of others. But for us who believe on Jesus, we'll never have to suffer the wrath of God. All that we suffer is sifted through God's love. People who reject Jesus as their Savior have to suffer God's wrath because of their sins.

But our Savior Jesus had to suffer both because of others and because the wrath of God the Father was poured out on Him. And none of His sufferings were *ever* deserved. Jesus didn't die on the cross because He had done something wrong. He died in our place because we would have died in our sins apart from Him.

Meditate with me on where we were headed before God the Father drew us to His Son. I believe the more we understand how truly wonderful salvation from hell is, the more gladness will grip our hearts.

Those who do not know God are separated from Him as His enemies. What a scary place to be! Those who refuse the forgiveness of sins God offers in Christ Jesus will have to give an account of all their deeds to God. God will judge sinners so accurately for their deeds that Jesus says in Matthew 12:36, "I tell you, on the day of judgment people will give account for every careless word they speak."

The God who never grows weary will not become wearied on Judgment Day either (Isaiah 40:28). God will repay the offenders for their deeds, as they deserve. Hebrews 9:27 says that "it is appointed for man to die once, and after that comes judgment."

How blessed we are to escape this wrath! Now if you're reading this and you realize you've never really come to God, or you've come with only your own righteousness, by believing in Jesus as your Lord and Savior you can have the righteousness of Christ imputed to you.

Please do not harden your heart if you realize you are guilty before God. God can declare your innocence through Jesus Christ if you will come to Him by faith. If you're not sure of your election, the Bible says that you need to "be all the more diligent to make your calling and election sure" (2 Peter 1:10). It is God's exceeding kindness toward you that allows you to be warned of judgment while there is still time to repent.

Now for those of us who have come to God by faith in Jesus, there is no need to doubt our salvation. One of the most reassuring verses in the Bible can be found in Hebrews 10:39, which says, "But we are not of those who shrink back and are destroyed, but of those who have faith and preserve their souls."

We can have so much joy that our souls have been preserved, by God's grace. Our names have been written in the book of life. These next verses in the book of Revelation speak of the immense benefit of having our names written in the book of life. They can be hard to swallow, so let yourself chew them over slowly in your mind, remembering how gracious God has been in choosing you for salvation:

> Then I saw a great white throne and him who was seated on it. From his presence earth and sky fled away, and no place was found for them. And I saw the dead, great and

small, standing before the throne, and books were opened. Then another book was opened, which is the book of life. And the dead were judged by what was written in the books, according to what they had done. And the sea gave up the dead who were in it, Death and Hades gave up the dead who were in them, and they were judged, each one of them, according to what they had done. Then Death and Hades were thrown into the lake of fire. This is the second death, the lake of fire. And if anyone's name was not found written in the book of life, he was thrown into the lake of fire.

(Revelation 20:11-15)

The lake of fire, which will be the eternal dwelling place of all those whose names are not written in the book of life, is a horrifying place. We learn from the words of Jesus in Mark 9:43 that this place of torment is eternal and the fire is never quenched. "It is a fearful thing to fall into the hands of the living God" (Hebrews 10:31).

Before God redeemed us, we also, like those who are perishing, had only the lake of fire to expect after death. We were guilty of having broken the whole law (James 2:10) and we were the slaves of sin (Romans 6:20). And to top it off, we were completely unable to do what is good and right. Paul writes in Romans 3:10-12, saying,

> As it is written:
> "None is righteous, no, not one;
> no one understands;
> no one seeks for God.
> All have turned aside; together they have become worthless;
> no one does good,
> not even one."

But what might appear sad is really stunningly beautiful. It may seem sad that we never sought God on our own, but it's a spectacular reality that in our depravity God still came and sought us. "In this is love, not that we have loved God but that he loved us and sent his Son to be the propitiation for our sins" (1 John 4:10).

We can rejoice in considering our former state because we are in that condition no longer. God, in His exceeding kindness and mercy toward us, made a way for us to be pleasing to Him. This is what made the cross necessary.

THE CELEBRATION OF GAINING CHRIST'S RIGHTEOUSNESS

Now let's consider together the sacrifice that the Lord Jesus Christ made on the cross, and the events leading up to it, so that we can celebrate together how great our salvation truly is. God sent His only begotten Son Jesus to be the complete and final sacrifice for sin (Hebrews 10:12). He was in the beginning with God, and He was God. All things were made by Him, and yet He humbled Himself and became a man on this earth around two thousand years ago. He lived blamelessly on this earth, although He was tempted at every point (Hebrews 4:15). Jesus was the only sinless person at any time throughout all history.

Then at the time appointed by God the Father, Jesus was crucified brutally on a cross and the wrath of God was poured out on Him. He was beaten, mocked, whipped, and then He died as He hung on that cross. Hebrews 12:2 says He despised the shame, yet He submitted Himself to the will of His Father. Isaiah 50:5-6 brings more clarity to this point: "The Lord GOD has opened my ear, and I was not rebellious; I turned not backward. I gave my back to those who strike, and my cheeks to those who pull out the beard; I hid not my face from disgrace and spitting."

The punishment Jesus endured for our sin was atrocious. His death was a death fitting for the worst of criminals, and yet Jesus was absolutely sinless. "God made him who had no sin to be sin for us, so that in him we might become the righteousness of God" (2 Corinthians 5:21 NIV). It wasn't because Jesus had done something wrong that He had to die for us.

Instead, it was the plan of God that through His Son salvation would come to sinners.

Before Adam and Eve had ever glanced at the appetizing fruit hanging from the tree of the knowledge of good and evil, God had already known they would sin. And God had made provision for sin to be forgiven before He even created Adam. While Eve listened intently to the serpent's persuasive attempt to make her eat what God had forbidden, and while Adam was willingly taking hold of the fruit God had commanded him against, it had already been determined that Jesus would suffer and die.

God the Father had foreordained that salvation would be purchased at the vast expense of the death of His Son. Jesus "was foreknown before the foundation of the world but was made manifest in the last times for your sake" (1 Peter 1:20). He was "delivered up according to the definite plan and foreknowledge of God" (Acts 2:23).

As the time grew near that Jesus was going to be crucified, He sweat great drops of blood. Large, heavy drops of warm red blood were coming from the very pores of the holy Son of God! Part of satiating God's wrath meant Jesus had to suffer shame, beatings, whippings, and crucifixion on a cross. He had to endure the holy wrath of the holy God poured upon Him in the fierceness of God's fiery anger.

As God poured His wrath upon His only begotten Son, Jesus cried out saying "'Eloi, Eloi, lema sabachthani?' which means, 'My God, my God, why have you forsaken me?'" (Mark 15:34). Jesus had to die as a man, separated from His Father, with whom He was one, so that we might come to God now through Him. I cannot imagine any greater cause of grief than separation from God. And the relationship between God the Father and God the Son was perfect, eternal, without flaw, and consisting of perfect love.

Now I want us to pause at the cross of Jesus and rewind back to the time of the Old Testament, when God allowed animal sacrifices to cover sin for a time. There is a great purpose for blood. Before scientists had ever discovered how important blood is for keeping a person alive, transporting oxygen and nutrients to the whole body, removing wastes, and healing infections, God declared that blood was necessary for life. "For the life of the flesh is in the blood, and I have given it for you on the altar to make atonement for your souls, for it is the blood that makes atonement by the life" (Leviticus 17:11).

Blood is both physically and spiritually necessary. Only through blood can sins ever be removed. Before Jesus died on the cross, the Jews who followed God sacrificed animals to atone for their sin. Not only does blood make an atonement for sins, but without blood and death there can be no atonement (Hebrews 9:22). Nothing else is sufficient.

So even before the death of Jesus, blood needed to be shed to cover the sins of God's people. Animal sacrifices fulfilled that obligation in part. However, the blood of animals only atoned for sins temporarily, "for it is impossible for the blood of bulls and goats to take away sins" (Hebrews 10:4). These animal sacrifices did their job for a time, but they couldn't do what was really necessary, and that was remove sin completely.

Now I want us to notice a distinct difference between animal sacrifices and the death of Jesus. Concerning animal sacrifices, God took no pleasure in them. Concerning the death of His own Son, God was very pleased. Part of this mystery is revealed in Isaiah 53:10, which says, "Yet it pleased the LORD to bruise [Jesus]." That word *pleased* is also commonly translated *delight*. God was pleased that His Son suffered, but God took no pleasure in the sacrifices of the animals. "In burnt offerings and sin offerings you have taken no pleasure" (Hebrews 10:6). Does this mean God loves animals more than His Son? Never! Rather, God was pleased to bruise His Son because He knew what the result would be.

Because Jesus died on the cross, no other sacrifice would ever be needed. "But when Christ had offered for all time a single sacrifice for sins, he sat down at the right hand of God" (Hebrews 10:12). Jesus was God's sacrifice who would take away sins once for all for everyone who would believe on Him.

Three days after He was crucified, Mary and the women who followed Jesus went to the tomb where He had been laid. The giant stone that had been put in front of the tomb (so the disciples of Jesus couldn't steal His body) had been rolled away. When the women arrived, they entered the tomb, but they did not see the body of Jesus. Instead they saw two men in shining garments.

"And as they were frightened and bowed their faces to the ground, the men said to them, 'Why do you seek the living among the dead? He is not here, but has risen. Remember how he told you, while he was still in Galilee, that the Son of Man must be delivered into the hands of sinful men and be crucified and on the third day rise.' And they remembered his words" (Luke 24:5-8). As they remembered His words, I wonder if there was a moment when they thought, "How did we forget *this*? Jesus told us He was going to *rise from the dead*, and we just forgot. What else have we forgotten?"

After this, Jesus was seen by His disciples and by over five hundred others (1 Corinthians 15:6). He stayed on earth for forty days after His resurrection, and then ascended up to heaven in the presence of His disciples. Jesus now sits at the right hand of the throne of God in heaven. Because Jesus has ascended to heaven, we have received the Holy Spirit to seal and dwell in us.

After Jesus rose from the dead, God highly exalted Him. His name is now and forever above every name (Philippians 2:9). Listen to how Jesus is described: "He is the radiance of the glory of God and the exact imprint of his nature, and he upholds the universe by the word of his power. After making purification for sins, he sat down at the right hand of the Majesty on high." Jesus, by Himself, purged our sins and was made sin for us. But Jesus is no longer on the cross. He rose from the dead.

And His righteousness has been imputed to us through believing. This righteousness has been "counted to us who believe in him who raised from the dead Jesus our Lord, who was delivered up for our trespasses and raised for our justification" (Romans 4:24-25). God showed His love to us through this, because it was while we were still sinners that Christ died for us. Since we have believed in Him, we have been justified by His blood and saved from God's wrath through Him (Romans 5:8-9).

"But thanks be to God, that you who were once slaves of sin have become obedient from the heart to the standard of teaching to which you were committed, and, having been set free from sin, have become slaves of righteousness" (Romans 6:17-18). Rejoice that the righteousness of Christ has been imputed to you! If any woman could completely understand that the *righteousness of God* has been bestowed upon her, I doubt that she could ever stop rejoicing! Our sins have been purged by Jesus Christ, and now we have boldness to enter God's presence, because Jesus has made a way for us through His blood. What a cause for holy delight!

~4~

Killing the Joy Thief

Since we have these promises, beloved, let us cleanse ourselves from every defilement of body and spirit, bringing holiness to completion in the fear of God.
2 Corinthians 7:1

Having laid the foundation of all true joy, let's now discuss sin, specifically relating to its consequences, because sin's consequences are severe, and they will stifle joy faster than water to a flame. The purpose of this is twofold: first, it's important to understand the destruction that results in us because of sin; second, understanding sin's destruction exhorts us to walk blamelessly, which will bring us to truly experiencing real joy.

Sin is the ultimate joy sapper. The more sin, the less joy. The more we walk in obedience to God and in fellowship with Him, the more our joy will be increased. If fullness of joy is in God's holy presence, then we can understand sin will remove us far from the source of joy, resulting in misery and harsh destruction.

Sin brings forth death. Sin will deaden your senses and rob your joy. Just like knowing the consequences of fire will motivate people to avoid letting their houses catch on fire, so knowing the harm sin produces in pilfering joy will supply motivation to avoid sin more actively.

In Psalm 38, David writes about the displeasure and grief he experienced in God's wrath. Part of this anguish was a result of his own sin, and in verses 3-6 David describes the consequences he endured as a direct result of his sin:

> There is no soundness in my flesh
> because of your indignation;
> there is no health in my bones
> because of my sin.
> For my iniquities have gone over my head;
> like a heavy burden, they are too heavy for me.
> My wounds stink and fester
> because of my foolishness,
> I am utterly bowed down and prostrate;
> all the day I go about mourning.

David's sin resulted in the troubling of his soul. He went around mourning continually, and he groaned heavily under the load of his guilt. He understood the greatest cause of his misery was his own sin.

Sin is a heavy burden. Look at the picturesque description in Hebrews 12:1 of the hindrance of sin, and note the response we need to have: "Let us also lay aside every weight, and sin which clings so closely." The weight of our sin will eventually become heavier than we can bear. There is no place to blame God when we are loaded down with the sheaves we've reaped in iniquity, because it's the heaviness of what we've sown in transgressions that keeps us from pursuing after God and soaring upward. I believe a very large amount of earthly suffering is the result of sin, whether our own sin or another person's sin.

So many women are drowning in anguish because others have poured the waters of disappointments and hardships over them. Often women enter the waters of suffering with a blindfold on. They carelessly chase after a relationship with an ungodly man, or try to achieve an earthly standard, or flirt with a self-exalting thought life, only to find they're neck high in the ocean of misery with a rising tide. We think it'll be safe to float on the inner tube of temptation, flirting with the waters of sin but not quite diving in, and, suddenly, we find we're drowning with no shore in sight.

But what about when someone else is making us suffer? What about when the thing that's making us feel upset and overwhelmed is not our fault? Is it okay to stop rejoicing? I believe the Bible teaches the answer is no. We can't stop rejoicing, and doing so is evidence that we are not content to be where God has us, even if it's in a place of suffering.

Do you remember the story of Job? Job chose to worship God when all his children had just been killed! Though he felt the heart-wrenching grief that came with the loss of his own children, Job still blessed God's name and did not charge or accuse God of wrong (Job 1:20-21).

And I also believe (and know from experience, unfortunately) that trials usually become much harder when a woman indulges herself in the sin of unbelief or discontentment. My husband and I have certain differences as to what we prefer, as is common in any marriage. My husband prefers hamburgers while I would rather eat something healthier.

In my attempts to be a submissive wife, I don't always get my way. And when I have to "suffer" because things are going very differently from what I may have wanted or imagined, sometimes it's hard to feel happy. But if I let myself grumble when I don't get my way, it only makes things worse. When I choose to rejoice in the Lord and love my husband even when I'm not "pleased" with him, he's usually a lot more willing to give in. Even if he's not, it's sweet to know my heart is pure before the Lord.

A blameless heart before God makes the denial of bitterness worth it. Let me illustrate this with an example. When Jenny's roommate Riley began to borrow her clothing without asking, Jenny was gracious at first. Soon Jenny's clothes began disappearing, and she started noticing stains she knew weren't her own. Riley wasn't even apologetic, and Jenny began to get very bitter. She grew unthankful that God had given her a place to live and instead complained her clothes were being ruined. Rather than rejoicing she even had clothes to be ruined, she focused only on what was going wrong.

When Jenny realized how bitter she'd become, she decided to commit Riley to prayer, dedicating one day a week to secret fasting for her. It was tough, but God blessed Jenny for it by allowing her to care more about Riley's heart than clothes that didn't even have a soul. She also started seeing Riley show more of an interest in reading her Bible. Their relationship greatly improved, and Riley even began to ask every time she wanted to borrow clothes, returning them in perfect condition and offering to pay for them when she didn't.

Soon their strained friendship was saturated with sweetness, and Riley became one of Jenny's most faithful, godly friends. Because Jenny chose to rejoice instead of wallowing in her complaints, she gained a friend whose nurturing friendship became one of the highlights of her life.

Can you think of a tough situation you've experienced that would've been easier for you by waiting on the Lord more contently and by giving thanks, even though you couldn't see the outcome? Do you think not being content made the situation worse? Is there anything you could do to improve a current situation that you may have been unwilling to do?

I have been miserable at times because I was slack in giving thanks in everything. Instead of praising and trusting God in my times of waiting, I impatiently thought of ways to hurry the situation along, and it only made things worse. If Jenny had moved out because of bitterness, she would have lost the fruit in her life that only grew from a field of self-denial seeded with supplication and praise.

When a woman has been wronged, forgotten, or not considered in the way she would have liked, the biblical response is to receive it with joy. The only way to do this sincerely is by understanding the loving character of God, even when she sees no change in her situation.

The woman who seeks to satisfy herself and who considers her own desires as better than pleasing God (although probably not even acknowledging that she does this) will bring upon herself additional unnecessary suffering. For instance, if Jenny had continued to put more value on her perishing clothes than on pleasing the eternal God, she would have become more and more miserable. A woman who seeks her own gain and her own honor without considering the needs of others will be more easily upset and offended when things don't go her way.

When a woman finds all her satisfaction in God, and looks continually at Him, she will not be offended unless someone offends her Lord. Don't spend your time protecting yourself. Purpose in your heart to honor God and believe He is the righteous judge who will defend your cause against others, if need be.

Follow Christ and the example He set of how to rejoice regardless of circumstances by believing in God and what He has promised is to come. Instead of looking at the trials, look "to Jesus, the founder and perfecter of our faith, who for the joy that was set before him endured the cross, despising the shame, and is seated at the right hand of the throne of God" (Hebrews 12:2). Jesus Himself endured the suffering of crucifixion on a cross, the shame of man, and separation from His Father, yet looked steadfastly through it all to the joy set before Him.

When a woman doesn't worship the one true God alone, but instead pursues her own gods (the things she adores, admires, or longs for above pleasing Christ), she will come to misery. The Bible gives clear warning that she will have sorrow in Psalm 16:4, which says the sorrows of those who choose or hasten after another god will be multiplied. Again, according to Psalm 32:10, it is the wicked who will experience many sorrows: "Many sorrows [shall be] to the wicked: but he that trusteth in the LORD, mercy shall compass him about" (KJV). If you obsessively and idolatrously chase after something you want other than God, your sorrows will be multiplied.

Anything we seek for ourselves can be another god to us, whether it be a perfectly organized house, a certain change in our husband, a better financial position, even a ministry at our church. The evidence we've made something a god is that when we don't get what we want, our joy is diminished and we become angry or frustrated. If we are going to be content and happy in our earthly trials, it is only going to come by having an eternal perspective.

Jenny was, at first, making the condition of her clothing a god, and this pursuit began to suffocate all her freedom and gladness. Jenny's story is one example, but every sin imaginable could be an example of some kind, so I exhort you to relate your own struggles to what I'm saying. If we want to experience true joy we must sincerely seek God first and His righteousness. A life that is given over to its own pursuits and pleasures will instead be a life filled with sorrow.

Sin is like fire. Can a man take fire into his lap and not get burned (Proverbs 6:27)? So it is with sin. Fire is mesmerizing to watch, and looks beautiful to the eye. Sin can also appear very appealing. It seems pleasurable to the unlearned. Yet as with fire, if we partake of fire in any way we will be burned, and the end of fire on the human body would be death. If a man walked into a fire pit to be part of the fire, his body would eventually be burned to death.

And sin also, when it is full grown, brings forth death (James 1:15). When we give in to any sinful pleasure or sinful desire, it will always bring forth destruction. It will bring forth the death of our emotions. It will kill relationships, destroy marriages, ruin health, steal joy, devastate lives, and bring damage of every sort.

If you have been convicted, be quick to repent. God has commanded us to be holy, even as He is holy. Holiness is not only outward, but inward. Sin must be purged from even the most private thoughts. God sees everything, as Moses declared, saying, "You have set our iniquities before you, our secret sins in the light of your presence" (Psalm 90:8). Numbers 32:23 says, "and be sure your sin will find you out."

Now this is a double-sided coin. On one side, we know that God blots out the sins of His people and remembers them no more (Isaiah 43:25). On the other side, we know from the Scriptures that God knows everything, which would include even the sins we haven't yet committed.

Rather than be discouraged that God knows our sin, we can be encouraged because God is greater than our sin. "For whenever our heart condemns us, God is greater than our heart, and he knows everything" (1 John 3:20). So as Christians, we are dearly loved by God, and He is our refuge even when we're fleeing the onslaught of penalties we've incurred. God pays even our earthly fines. When we've racked up fees against earthly creditors, God can and does often pay those debts for us. Like David, God sometimes removes our enemies and destroys them on our behalf (2 Samuel 22:1-20).

But though God is gracious beyond our understanding, we cannot permit our sin so that grace may abound (Romans 6:1-2). The Bible gives us heavy words concerning sin and its consequences. Although God knows even the purposes of the heart, people disregard God when they only desire to cover their sins from others. They partake of their sin in secrecy, justify their transgressions while privately longing for them, and forget the infinite knowledge of the God in whose hands their very breath is. What a tragedy this is.

Now it makes sense this would be true of the unbeliever, but what about those who confess Christ as their Savior? How could a believer still long for sin? The Bible says that as believers, we are dead to sin. "How can we who died to sin still live in it?" (Romans 6:2). What understanding saint, at the time when her physical body dies, would choose for her spirit to stay with her dead flesh in the grave? Would she not rather leave her dead and rotting flesh in the grave where it was buried and receive with abundant gladness the new and glorified body that God has given her?

In the same way, wouldn't you rather leave the dead and rotting body of sin to walk in holiness and newness of life? We have such an advantage over unbelievers. They are the slaves of sin, but we have been freed from sin. It is still very possible for the believer to sin, but according to Romans 6:11, we are to reckon ourselves as dead to sin.

As we wait for the redemption of our bodies, we need to consider ourselves as already dead to sin. The more we present our bodies to righteousness, the more sanctified we will become. We must wholeheartedly consider our flesh as dead; we must *reckon* our flesh as dead! Paul explains it this way: "For you have died, and your life is hidden with Christ in God. When Christ who is your life appears, then you also will appear with him in glory. Put to death therefore what is earthly in you: sexual immorality, impurity, passion, evil desire, and covetousness, which is idolatry" (Colossians 3:3-5).

Is it still possible for the Christian to sin? Absolutely! But though it's *possible* for a Christian to sin, it is not in accordance with salvation for a person who names Christ to continue in sin. "Whoever says 'I know him' but does not keep his commandments is a liar, and the truth is not in him" (1 John 2:4).

We have no goodness of ourselves at all apart from the righteousness of Christ imputed to us. We should be deeply grieved, but not shocked, when a person is able to fall to the very depths of wickedness. Therefore it is imperative that we realize how frail we are and how capable we are in ourselves of committing blasphemous sin against God, so we can be on guard against these things.

The fallen man is dead *in* sin, and the redeemed man must reckon himself dead *to* sin. Our flesh has *positionally* been crucified with Christ. Romans 8:13 says, "For if you live according to the flesh you will die, but if by the Spirit you put to death the deeds of the body, you will live." By the Holy Spirit which dwells in us we are fully able to walk blamelessly and uprightly, putting to death all that is of our rebellious human nature towards God. This putting to death of what is earthly in us will allow the righteousness of God to flourish, making room for gladness to abound.

~5~

Drawing Near to God

You make known to me the path of life; in your presence there is fullness of joy; at your right hand are pleasures forevermore.

Psalm 16:11

We've looked at the root of joy, which is making Jesus the Lord of our life, and we've looked at how sin will eat away at that root and decrease our production of joy. Now let's see how our continuing relationship with God will be our sustaining spring of gladness. The Bible actually says there are certain specific behaviors and ways that, if a person does them, will produce a harvest of joy. This chapter begins the study of twenty-two of those ways.

JOY COMES FROM BEING FILLED WITH THE HOLY SPIRIT

Joy is the natural manifestation of a person filled with the Holy Spirit. Without the Holy Spirit there can be no fullness of joy. Earthly delight is fleeting and is caused by temporal events. Heavenly joy is eternal, caused by immovable and unchangeable truths that will never fade or weaken.

Galatians 5:22 says, "The fruit of the Spirit is […] joy." People who lack joy evidence by their actions they are not filled with the Holy Spirit.

A Christian woman who abounds in genuine, unwavering joy demonstrates by her behavior she is likely being influenced by the Holy Spirit. (This doesn't mean a woman can't be sorrowful, but there will be an undercurrent of joy in her life that is stronger than every wave of trials that crash upon her.)

In the same way, apples growing from a branch would be the proof of an apple tree. If an "apple" tree produced oranges, we would know it was really not an apple tree but an orange tree. The evidence that a person is filled with the Holy Spirit is the fruit of love, joy, peace, patience, kindness, goodness, gentleness, faith, and self-control (Galatians 5:22).

Think about these "fruits" of the Spirit. Do you exemplify these things in your own life? If one or more of these characteristics are not part of your life, consider why. If you are a believer, the Holy Spirit of God does dwell inside you, but it is possible to suppress the Spirit. Just like we can stifle a fire by throwing dirt upon it, so we can quench the work of God's Spirit in our life.

First Thessalonians 5:19 says, "Do not quench the Spirit." Dear sister, do not suppress the Holy Spirit. He works in us, sanctifying us so we abound in righteousness. When the fruit of the Spirit is not evident in a person's life, there are two possibilities. The first is that the Spirit is being quenched. Allow room for the Holy Spirit to do what He wants in your life by obeying the commandments of God.

The other option is much worse. If a person consistently does not demonstrate the fruit of the Spirit, he may not be truly saved. I say this because 1 John 2:4 says, "Whoever says 'I know him' but does not keep his commandments is a liar, and the truth is not in him." If a person claims to know God, but they do not obey what God has commanded, then according to Scripture that person is lying. He does not truly know God.

Many times, when I have been witnessing, people alienated from God will say they wouldn't want to be Christian because of the "hypocrites." My response has been that anyone can *say* he is a Christian, but a true Christian will act like a Christian. Don't believe everyone who claims to be a Christian. The evidence of true Christians will be the fruits they bear, just like the obvious evidence of an apple tree is the apples it produces.

The second fruit of the Spirit, joy, will be evidence the Holy Spirit dwells in you. Apart from the Holy Spirit, a person cannot truly abound with the fruit of the Spirit. Jesus said in John 15:4-5, "Abide in me, and I in you. As the branch cannot bear fruit by itself, unless it abides in the vine, neither can you, unless you abide in me. I am the vine; you are the branches. Whoever abides in me and I in him, he it is that bears much fruit, for apart from me you can do nothing."

In the same way the branches depend upon the vine or trunk for their life and sustenance, so we must depend upon God to bear fruit. And just like a branch broken off from the tree will die and won't produce fruit, so we also can do nothing apart from the Lord. If you want to abound with joy in your life, then abide in the vine, Jesus, and do not quench God's Spirit.

JOY COMES FROM SALVATION

The Bible says in several ways that joy comes from salvation. The word *salvation* means "preservation or deliverance from destruction, difficulty, or evil." In the verses we'll be looking at from the Old Testament, salvation is usually referring to deliverance from difficulty. In the New Testament, the word *salvation* usually refers to the salvation of our souls from sin, death, hell, and the lake of fire. In both cases, salvation will bring us joy, whether we are saved from immediate earthly danger or future eternal punishment.

David records, in a very thought-provoking verse, how God's salvation has effected his emotions, saying, "O LORD, in your strength the king rejoices, and in your salvation how greatly he exults!" (Psalm 21:1-2). David rejoiced because God had given him salvation.

We can rejoice through trusting in God because He is both strong and faithful. Just like David, the prophet Isaiah also rejoiced as he put his trust in God. Because he was confident that God would save him, he joyfully proclaimed that the Lord was his salvation in Isaiah 12:2-3, saying,

> "Behold, God is my salvation;
> I will trust, and will not be afraid;
> for the LORD GOD is my strength and my song,
> and he has become my salvation."
> With joy you will draw water from the wells of salvation.

Since it is the Lord who is our strength, we joyfully draw water out of the wells of salvation. For us in the new covenant today, God is both our salvation in whom we are safe, and our salvation in whom we are saved. If we have trusted the Lord for our eternal security, how much more should we trust Him as our temporal refuge? If God can save us from hell, He can surely deliver us from our enemies, our emotional frustrations, and the mistakes we've made, as He sees fit.

Faith in God is the antidote for alarming and daunting fears. As we trust the One who can surely save us, making God our shelter both in this life and in the life to come, frightful doubting is replaced with glorified rejoicing.

Think of the times when you've experienced the salvation of God in your life. If you have ever avoided a car accident, that's evidence of God's salvation and mercy toward you. Maybe God has faithfully delivered you financially, or preserved your health, or kept you from trouble.

When God shows Himself strong on a woman's behalf, and saves her, that is a great cause for gladness. When your heart despairs, take time to consider and thank God for everything you have to be thankful for. Thanking God is the harmony that gives joy richness and depth.

A third note that can make the symphony of joy so enchanting is knowing that, even when things may be difficult, God hears the cries of His people. David rejoiced at God's salvation even when he was still waiting for it:

> But I am afflicted and in pain;
> let your salvation, O God, set me on high!
> I will praise the name of God with a song;
> I will magnify him with thanksgiving.
> This will please the LORD more than an ox
> or a bull with horns and hoofs.
> When the humble see it they will be glad;
> you who seek God, let your hearts revive.
> For the LORD hears the needy
> and does not despise his own people who are prisoners.
> Let heaven and earth praise him,
> the seas and everything that moves in them.
> (Psalm 69:29-34)

Notice the first three lines: because David was afflicted and in pain, he would *praise God*? How often do we say, "Because I am enduring these difficult trials, because I am in so much pain, therefore I will praise God, sing to Him, magnify Him, and thank Him!"? Even though David was afflicted and in pain, he allowed just the thought of God's salvation to revive his heart and compel him to magnify the Lord with thanksgiving.

Praising God with a song and magnifying Him with thanksgiving pleases God. It glorifies Him. When we feel discouraged, by praising God for His past deliverances in our lives, our discouragement can be traded for joyful anticipation. God is always faithful. He has given every believer multitudes upon multitudes of reasons to be thankful and to rejoice in Him.

Psalm 116:6-8 says, "The LORD preserves the simple; when I was brought low, he saved me. Return, O my soul, to your rest; for the LORD has dealt bountifully with you. For you have delivered my soul from death, my eyes from tears, my feet from stumbling." Unlike our rejoicing at the cross of Christ by faith, we rejoice at the salvation of God in temporal events by sight. The psalmist saw God's salvation when he proclaimed that God had delivered his feet from falling.

Oh, the times God has delivered my feet from falling! God who is both eternal and unchangeable so often preserves us in both things we see and do not see. Every time I'm preserved from sinning, it is God who has delivered my feet from falling. He alone enables us to walk pleasing to Him, and He is worthy of your song, because He delivers your soul from death, your eyes from tears, and your feet from falling!

God delivers us and saves us, and He is worthy of grateful praise and rejoicing. Psalm 13:5-6 says, "But I have trusted in your steadfast love; my heart shall rejoice in your salvation. I will sing to the LORD, because he has dealt bountifully with me." In this verse we see the theme of singing mentioned again in the context of rejoicing over God's salvation. Do you sing to the Lord joyfully because of His salvation?

And the blessed thing is that as we sing joyfully to the Lord, He is also rejoicing over us with singing. Zephaniah 3:17 says, "The LORD your God is in your midst, a mighty one who will save; he will rejoice over you with gladness; he will quiet you by his love; he will exult over you with loud singing."

God has unlimited power to save us out of every trial in this life, but there may be times when He doesn't save us from our circumstances because He is doing a greater work than we may be able to see. It is in these times, when we don't see God delivering us from our hardships, that we must learn to rejoice in God's love, knowing He works all things together for our good. God has and will even use death to glorify Himself.

In John 11 there is a story about a friend of Jesus named Lazarus who got very sick. When Jesus was told about the sickness of Lazarus, He didn't immediately heal him. Instead of promptly traveling to Bethany where Lazarus was dying, Jesus stayed where He was for two more days. While Jesus was purposely waiting to leave, Lazarus died. Would Jesus have been able to heal Lazarus if He had left sooner? Absolutely. Would He have been able to heal Lazarus by just speaking the word for Lazarus to be healed, as in the case of the centurion's servant (Matthew 8:13)? Yes!

Is God able to deliver you out of every trial you're currently in? Without a doubt! So if God can save you from every trial in this life, why wouldn't He? I believe the answer is found in the story of Lazarus. Read carefully what the answer of Jesus was to those who gave Him the news about Lazarus' sickness: "It is for the glory of God, so that the Son of God may be glorified through it" (John 11:4). Did you notice Jesus' reason for Lazarus' sickness? Lazarus was sick so God would be glorified.

After Lazarus died, Jesus told His disciples, "and for your sake *I am glad that I was not there*, so that you may believe. But let us go to him" (John 11:15, italics added). Even though Jesus knew Lazarus had died, He was still happy He was not there, because He knew the end result would bring glory to God. All that Jesus did was with a purpose: to bring glory to God His Father. Jesus stated His intention to bring God glory shortly before going to the cross, when He prayed to the Father, "I glorified you on earth, having accomplished the work that you gave me to do" (John 17:4).

When Jesus did finally arrive in Bethany, Lazarus had been dead four days. When Martha heard that Jesus was coming, she went out to meet Him. Jesus told her His plan: "Your brother will rise again" (John 11:23). She did not understand that Jesus meant He was going to raise Lazarus from the dead. Then Mary came out to see Him, and when Jesus saw her and all the Jews weeping, He groaned within Himself and wept. As they came to the tomb, Jesus questioned Martha: "Did I not tell you that if you believed you would see the glory of God?" (John 11:40).

After praying, Jesus cried with a loud voice, "Lazarus, come out" (John 11:43). Then Lazarus, who had been dead, came out, bound completely with grave clothes. He that was dead had been made alive! What was the result of this? "Many of the Jews therefore, who had come with Mary and had seen what he did, believed in him" (John 11:45). Rather than healing Lazarus without delay, Jesus intentionally allowed him to die so He could raise him from the dead. God was glorified in this miracle, and many of the Jews who saw what Jesus did believed on Him.

Can you see how this story might relate to your own situation? Just as God delayed His answer to Lazarus for greater glory, God might not always save you in this life, in order to accomplish a greater glory. Although I don't want to try to explain exactly what God is doing, may I suggest what I personally believe is often the case? When you trust God in the midst of difficult situations, He receives greater glory than if you were spared from all difficulty. It's possible that God is glorified more when you rejoice in tribulations then if you were to rejoice in everything going well.

Therefore be strong in the Lord and in the power of His might, resisting the temptation to sin against God through unbelief. Instead of doubting God's concern for you when He doesn't act immediately and your desires seem to go unfulfilled, instead trust that God is working things together for a greater glory. Rejoice by faith that God will be your strength and your song, and that He will save you when He knows that is best.

And whether or not you can see it, God has dealt bountifully with you. God has dealt bountifully with every believer at all times because it will be well for them on the day of God's judgment. This life may or may not abound with "bounty," but the end is always good, and so God has dealt bountifully with us. God's goodness toward us on the day of judgment, whether or not this life has anything we think we want, is enough reason for us to glorify God with rejoicing forever!

This means we always have an occasion to rejoice in our salvation that is yet to come. Paul says in Romans 5:11, "More than that, we also rejoice in God through our Lord Jesus Christ, through whom we have now received reconciliation." We rejoice through Jesus Christ because in Him we have received reconciliation with God. We have been made right with God, and on the day we stand before Him it will be well with our soul because of Christ's righteousness.

Eternal salvation, which is obtained through faith in Jesus, and which seals us with the Holy Spirit, and is worked out by us with fear and trembling, is cause for great holy rejoicing. Even among the angels there is rejoicing over salvation! In Luke 15:10 Jesus says, "Just so, I tell you, there is joy before the angels of God over one sinner who repents." Even the angels rejoice when they see God working eternal salvation in the lives of the elect. We have so many reasons to rejoice at God's salvation. He displays His salvation in so many things, and we are the blessed benefactors. So rejoice!

GOD HIMSELF IS OUR JOY

Even more than what God *does* for us, He Himself is the greatest joy a woman can ever have. Psalm 43:4 says, "Then I will go to the altar of God, to God my exceeding joy." According to this verse, our exceeding joy is not a thing, but a person. Fullness of joy is found in the very presence of God. Psalm 16:11 says, "You make known to me the path of life; in your presence there is fullness of joy; at your right hand are pleasures forevermore."

Glorified joy in its fullness cannot be achieved apart from God. Take a moment to really consider the greatness of God. God Himself can be and should be the greatest joy we have ever known. A person who lacks joy lacks God, and there can be no true joy apart from God.

As the redeemed of the Lord, we can enjoy intimate fellowship with Him, who made all the heavens by His spoken word: "By the word of the LORD the heavens were made, and by the breath of his mouth all their host" (Psalm 33:6). Jeremiah acknowledged the greatness of God saying,

> Ah Lord GOD! behold, thou hast made the heaven and the earth by thy great power and stretched out arm, [and] there is nothing too hard for thee:… the Great, the Mighty God, the LORD of hosts, [is] his name, Great in counsel, and mighty in work […] Behold, I [am] the LORD, the God of all flesh: is there any thing too hard for me? (Jeremiah 32:17-19, 27 KJV).

The answer is there is nothing too hard for the Lord. His eyes are open upon all the ways of the sons of men, and even in the excellency of His greatness God considers us. When we realize how great our God is, it makes His intimate knowledge of us all the more mind-blowing.

Sometimes it's hard to believe that a God who is so grand and glorious, who only had to speak and the heavens were formed, could be more familiar and aware of us than we are of ourselves. But see what David says to the Lord concerning God's personal and caring concern for us:

> O LORD, you have searched me and known me!
> You know when I sit down and when I rise up;
> you discern my thoughts from afar.
> You search out my path and my lying down
> and are acquainted with all my ways.
> Even before a word is on my tongue,
> behold, O LORD, you know it altogether…
> How precious to me are your thoughts, O God!
> How vast is the sum of them!
> If I would count them, they are more than the sand.
> I awake, and I am still with you.
> (Psalm 139:1-4, 17-18)

The exceedingly all-powerful, all-knowing God considers us! He is knowledgeable about all that we do. He knows when we are sad. He puts our tears in a bottle. Psalm 56:8 says, "You have kept count of my tossings; put my tears in your bottle. Are they not in your book?" He sees our every tear, our sleeplessness, our longings, and He has numbered every hair on our head.

God is so in control of all things that not even a bird can fall to the ground and die unless He allows it. Jesus said "Are not two sparrows sold for a penny? And not one of them will fall to the ground apart from your Father. But even the hairs of your head are all numbered. Fear not, therefore; you are of more value than many sparrows" (Mark 10:29-31). If we are of more value than many sparrows, and one sparrow can't even die unless God allows it, do you think any one of us would be able to die unless God allowed it?

All that comes into our lives is as God has allowed. Knowing this is more necessary than I can communicate if you want to be steadfastly joyful. I *must* fall back on God's sovereignty (His perfect control of all things) when I want to dwell in disappointment over a situation. I can't imagine being a happy woman if I thought my God wasn't able or didn't want to take care of me in all things.

So much joy and contentment in my own life come from resting in God's love combined with His sovereignty. When I want something and I don't get it, I can say with all confidence, "Thank You Lord! That was from Your hand and it was good because You're working everything in my life together for good!"

For many years I longed to teach the Bible to women and God did not fulfill my request. Not being able to have this request brought me many times of tearfully asking the Lord why He'd placed such a strong desire in my heart without fulfilling it. But after I'd cried out to the Lord, and received no positive answer to my request, I had a choice. I could complain about why it wasn't happening, or rejoice in God's sovereignty and acknowledge it is God in His *goodness* who had withheld this from me.

I don't for a moment think teaching was withheld from me because God couldn't give it, or that He was unaware I wanted it—but because God's timing was perfect, He withheld my request to satisfy His perfect timing.

While I was waiting, I learned to want God's will above *every* desire of my heart and I became willing to sacrifice all my desires if it meant being pleasing to God. This is when understanding God's sovereignty became my sweetest friend, and I was able to rest even with unfulfilled desire because I know my God is good, kind, loving, and wise beyond the heavens.

Instead of grumbling, I had to realize God's grace alone is sufficient for me (2 Corinthians 12:9). And then, in God's perfect timing, He did open the door for me to begin teaching—and I can see even more clearly that it's not teaching but God's grace alone that is sufficient for me.

Dear lovely sister, instead of dwelling on the trials, dwell on the greatness of God! Though I had to wait for over a decade with intense craving, I can see now how, in God's infinite wisdom, He knew when it would be best for my desire to be fulfilled. And I praise God for His goodness toward me in not giving me what I wanted right when I wanted it. I don't want to imagine what would have happened if He had!

If you're waiting for something in your life to change or happen, don't get so caught up in your desire that you lose sight of God's wisdom and goodness. If you search for your happiness in situations, there's no guarantee you'll ever find any. If you search for your happiness in God Himself, giving yourself to Him for His glory, you will always come up drenched in His joy. Trusting God regardless of your circumstances is crucial; if you only trust God when your circumstances are good, you are never really trusting Him.

And it's not because a woman is a mighty spiritual giant that she trusts and loves God, but because she has simply understood how much God loves her and how concerned He really is with her. "We love because he first loved us" (1 John 4:19).

The more we understand by faith how much God cares about us, the easier it will be for us to increase in our own love for Him. Do you find it easy or hard to genuinely believe and receive the truth about God's intimate care and concern for you? The more we receive His love by faith and choose to believe that God intimately knows and loves us, the more our love for Him will also be increased. Jesus assured His eleven disciples of God's love (after Judas had gone out), the way we who love God are also assured of His love for us. "For the Father himself loves you, because you have loved me and have believed that I came from God" (John 16:27).

God's love for us is so much greater than human love, and He wants us to know and understand this love! The prayer of the Holy Spirit for us through Paul was that we might understand the love of Christ: "So that Christ may dwell in your hearts through faith—that you, being rooted and grounded in love, may have strength to comprehend with all the saints what is the breadth and length and height and depth, and to know the love of Christ that surpasses knowledge, that you may be filled with all the fullness of God" (Ephesians 3:17-19). God's desire for you is that you might fully comprehend His love for you and be filled with all of His fullness. Wow!

God's love for us is revealed again in John 14:21, which says, "Whoever has my commandments and keeps them, he it is who loves me. And he who loves me will be loved by my Father, and I will love him and manifest myself to him." God has both loved you from one end of eternity to the other, and then at this present moment in time He delights to draw you to Himself with lovingkindness.

The God who inhabits eternity, whose name is holy, and who is God even from everlasting to everlasting, knows your name, and delights in you. The mighty, righteous, faithful, true, living God who alone has immortality and exists both now and eternally, and whose presence spans all time, be glorified, because He has chosen to set His love upon *you*! If this doesn't make you smile, then please reread the verses in this chapter until you do smile! Believe what God's Word says, because His love for us is our life!

In response to God's love, I want to agree with those who have proclaimed God's awesomeness. Read the following words of worship with the same passion the authors must have had when they penned the words:

> "To the King of ages, immortal, invisible, the only God, be honor and glory forever and ever. Amen" (1 Timothy 1:17).

> "To the only God, our Savior, through Jesus Christ our Lord, be glory, majesty, dominion, and authority, before all time and now and forever. Amen" (Jude 1:25).

> "Oh, the depth of the riches and wisdom and knowledge of God! How unsearchable are his judgments and how inscrutable his ways!" (Romans 11:33).

> "Yours, O LORD, is the greatness and the power and the glory and the victory and the majesty, for all that is in the heavens and in the earth is yours. Yours is the kingdom, O LORD, and you are exalted as head above all" (1 Chronicles 29:11).
>
> "Worthy are you, our Lord and God, to receive glory and honor and power, for you created all things, and by your will they existed and were created" (Revelation 4:11).
>
> "And I heard every creature in heaven and on earth and under the earth and in the sea, and all that is in them, saying, 'To him who sits on the throne and to the Lamb be blessing and honor and glory and might forever and ever!'" (Revelation 5:13-14).

We are so blessed to be loved by the only true God. Our God sits in majesty and glory and honor and strength on the throne of His glory. He is altogether glorious and His glory is eternal. Jesus the Lamb of God and the Father upon the throne are worthy of blessing, honor, glory, and power.

Oh, how necessary it is that you come to God by faith, believing that He is the eternal God who calls you by name and has numbered all the hairs on your head. Trust in the One who has known your name for all eternity and loves you with an everlasting love. Rejoice in the God who also rejoices over you with joy and singing.

Meditate on the Scriptures that God has given you that speak of His concern and love for you, His child. "Faith comes by hearing, and hearing by the word of God" (Romans 10:17 KJV). Hearing the Word of God brings salvation, but our faith is also increased as we know and understand the Bible more deeply. The depth of the relationship you have with the God who is love will determine the steadfastness of your joy in Him. As you understand and know Him more you will experience greater and greater joy. In His presence is fullness of joy, so enter into His presence with thanksgiving and praise in your heart, and *rejoice*!

~6~

Will Work for Joy

Addressing one another in psalms and hymns and spiritual songs, singing and making melody to the Lord with all your heart, giving thanks always and for everything to God the Father in the name of our Lord Jesus Christ.
Ephesians 5:19-20

*U*ntil now, we've been learning to pursue God, who is the only course to finding real gladness. He is still and always will be the only route, and the course is not about finding joy but finding God, with joy being the afterglow, if you will. What the Bible says about attaining joy is based in pleasing God and bringing Him glory.

Each point I make on obtaining joy has at least one verse, if not many more, on which my point stands. I can promise that if you do all the things I talk about in this book daily, you will be a joyful (and definitely not bored) woman! Knowing that all true happiness is from the Lord's hand alone, we recognize it's through God's holy and inspired Word we will obtain our understanding.

The activities in this chapter are categorized as physical labors because they take some degree of bodily activity. The measures I'm urging you to take require more than just mental work, but you must actually do something with your physical self to find joy in these areas. Most of these things are not strenuous labors, but even the activities of reading the Bible or prayer take a degree of work, commitment, and endurance.

In our pursuit of glorious and inexpressible joy, which is really our pursuit of God ("rejoice *in the Lord* always" Philippians 4:4, [italics added]), we will examine the seedlings that, if grown diligently, will cultivate a great crop of gladness in our lives.

GOD'S WORD BRINGS JOY

The Bible is filled with the rejoicings of those who delighted themselves in God's Word. In Psalm 119, David repeatedly expressed his own joy over God's testimonies, His precepts, His ways, His statutes, His commandments, His judgments, His Word, and His law. David's first mention of his delight at God's Word in this psalm is powerful, as he equates his joy over God's Word with riches, saying, "In the way of your testimonies I delight as much as in all riches" (Psalm 119:14).

When we compare this verse to our own life, we are most likely humbled by our lack of joy over the Bible! Compare your joy the last time you opened the Bible and read it to the reaction you'd have if you found out you'd won a $134,000,000 lottery two minutes ago. Upon receiving so much money, there's a good chance you'd be gushing with excitement, jumping, screaming, and telling the people you love. Was this the same reaction you had to the Word of God the last time you read it?

David said that he rejoiced in God's Word as much as in all riches. Our thought and emotion should be, *If I were given every dollar and valuable item in the world, I would rejoice more in the Word of God.* And God's Word is so much better than riches, because riches sprout wings and fly away (Proverbs 23:5), but the Word of God endures forever, gives life, and reveals God to us.

Rejoice in God's Word with the excitement you would have if you found an exceedingly valuable treasure. Psalm 119:162 says, "I rejoice at your word like one who finds great spoil." Know that the reading of God's

Word is truly one of the most exciting things you will ever do in your life. To those who are dead spiritually, this would be a revolting thought, because they cannot even understand the Bible. First Corinthians 2:14 says, "The natural person does not accept the things of the Spirit of God, for they are folly to him, and he is not able to understand them because they are spiritually discerned."

But to the spiritually discerned woman, understanding the Bible and eating the strong meat of the Word is more rewarding than the greatest earthly treasure. Through learning the Bible I am so aware of the advantage I have over those who are spiritually undiscerned. The knowledge of what God says has given me more understanding about what to do in even practical areas of life than those outside of faith in Christ. No wonder David said, "Your commandment makes me wiser than my enemies, for it is ever with me. I have more understanding than all my teachers, for your testimonies are my meditation. I understand more than the aged, for I keep your precepts" (Psalm 119:98-100).

The Word of God is truly more valuable than great treasure, and obtaining the understanding of it is one of the very pinnacles of all earthly joys. Psalm 119:111 says, "Your testimonies are my heritage forever, for they are the joy of my heart." God's Word, what the Holy Bible declares in all its truth and promises, is more valuable than any earthly inheritance. Because God's Word is capable of bringing such great delight and joy, David wanted it be his eternal inheritance. It is worth trading our portion and reward in this life for the good, true, and eternal promises of God.

David continues to express his delight in God's Word often throughout this chapter. Let's go through Psalm 119 together and read each verse about delighting in the Word of God:

> I will delight in your statutes;
> I will not forget your word. (Vs. 16)

> Your testimonies are my delight;
> they are my counselors. (Vs. 24)

> Lead me in the path of your commandments,
> for I delight in it. (Vs. 35)
>
> for I find my delight in your commandments,
> which I love. (Vs. 47)
>
> their heart is unfeeling like fat,
> but I delight in your law. (Vs. 70)
>
> Let your mercy come to me, that I may live;
> for your law is my delight. (Vs. 77)
>
> If your law had not been my delight,
> I would have perished in my affliction. (Vs. 92)
>
> Trouble and anguish have found me out,
> but your commandments are my delight. (Vs. 143)
>
> I long for your salvation, O LORD,
> and your law is my delight. (Vs. 174)

These nine verses exhort us by David's example to delight greatly at God's Word. The Word of God will sustain you in affliction. God's Word will keep you together in trials. David again speaks concerning God's Word and how it brings joy in Psalm 19:8, saying, "The precepts of the LORD are right, rejoicing the heart; the commandment of the LORD is pure, enlightening the eyes."

Jeremiah the prophet also expressed his delight at the Word of God in Jeremiah 15:16, saying, "Your words were found, and I ate them, and your words became to me a joy and the delight of my heart, for I am called by your name, O LORD, God of hosts." Jeremiah said he ate God's words. When we eat food it becomes a part of us, and in the same way when we read the Bible it needs to become part of us—and the joy and rejoicing of our heart!

We've seen David and Jeremiah's joy over God's Word. Paul also expresses his own delight in God's Word, saying in Romans 7:22, "For I delight in the law of God, in my inner being." By the Spirit of God that dwelt in him, Paul also found happiness in God's Word.

Now Jesus, who is God and who created all things, including us, and who knows our frame, says concerning joy: "These things I have spoken to you, that my joy may be in you, and that your joy may be full" (John 15:11). Jesus knows what is in man. He Himself made man, and He has shown us how we can have fullness of joy, even His very own joy; and He was anointed with the oil of gladness above all his companions (Hebrews 1:9).

Full means "containing as much as is possible; complete in extent or degree and in every particular." You cannot have any more joy than fullness of joy. It is by the Holy Bible that we learn *how* to experience being full of joy. Can you think of a time when you have been reading God's Word and a certain passage or verse spoke directly to your heart in such a way that you were filled with great joy?

God knows your life, He knows everything about you, and He is able to communicate directly to you by His Word. The Bible is alive, and God can make certain words jump off the page and touch us deeper than heart surgery.

Now, just as Jesus said that the things He spoke were for our joy, John also speaks on this theme of fullness of joy by the Word of God again, saying, "And these things write we unto you, that your joy may be full" (1 John 1:4 KJV). What an amazing statement! Parts of the Bible were written just so we could be happy and bring God glory through our joy? Yes! God's Word is meant to be an intense well of joy for us to draw from. Both having God's Word in its entirety and having specific Scriptures is reason for our rejoicing.

We know that God's Word is to be rejoiced in. But what characteristics does the Bible have that make the words so good, that even our human emotion of joy would be full? First, the Bible is inspired by God. Second Timothy 3:16-17 says, "All Scripture is breathed out by God and profitable for teaching, for reproof, for correction, and for training in righteousness, that the man of God may be competent, equipped for every good work." The Bible is without fault, because God Himself has inspired every word written in it.

Most of the Old Testament in its original language is in Hebrew, and the New Testament was written in Greek. The entire Bible was written by forty different authors, and consists of sixty-six books. God has preserved the Bible, and those who know Hebrew or Greek can read the same words now that were written thousands of years ago. God's power is not limited, and it's no harder for Him to preserve the original words of the Bible than it is for Him to do any other thing. I do believe that in studying the Bible it's important to research the meaning of words in their original language, and to not always take the translation of the Bible that you are reading for granted. But the Bible in its original languages is perfect and exact.

God has maintained the accuracy of the Bible. Isaiah 40:8 says, "The grass withers, the flower fades, but the word of our God will stand forever." Peter reiterates this thought by saying, "The word of the Lord remains forever. And this word is the good news that was preached to you" (1 Peter 1:25). God's Word will stand forever.

Another characteristic of the Bible is that it's *true*. How many deceptions and lies would you estimate that you're exposed to on a daily basis? Truth is valuable. And truth is rare. Think about how many times science has "changed" over the years. Consider how many advertisements promise more than what's often given. Truth is worth clinging to.

Proverbs 30:5 says, "Every word of God proves true." Again, Psalm 12:6 says, "The words of the LORD are pure words, like silver refined in a furnace on the ground, purified seven times." Psalm 18:30 says, "This God—his way is perfect; the word of the LORD proves true; he is a shield for all those who take refuge in him." We find what is accurate and truly right in the pages of the Bible. It is the ultimate reference for truth.

The Bible is also very powerful. Hebrews 4:12 says, "For the word of God is living and active, sharper than any two-edged sword, piercing to the division of soul and of spirit, of joints and of marrow, and discerning the thoughts and intentions of the heart." The Word of God can discern the thoughts of a woman's heart, and God uses the Bible to bring conviction.

Because God's commandments are holy, just, and good, they reveal our exceeding sinfulness to us. But God's Word is without fault, pure, refined, spiritual, holy, just, good, given by God's inspiration, profitable, living, powerful, and able to discern even the thoughts and intents of your heart! The words of God are alive and endure forever. Therefore it is very important to increase in your knowledge, understanding, obedience, and love of God's Word so that your joy may increase.

It's also important to be convinced of the benefit of the Word of God. We've seen how David, Jeremiah, and Paul all found their joy in God's Word. We've also looked at some weighty characteristics of the Bible.

Now let's briefly overview several benefits of God's Word. To start with, God's Word gives us life. Philippians 2:16 says, "Holding fast to the *word of life*, so that in the day of Christ I may be proud that I did not run in vain or labor in vain" (italics added). Notice here what the Bible is called. It's called the Word of *life*.

We must cling tightly to the words of God, which give life, so we can have joy on the day Christ returns. In John 6:63 Jesus says, "It is the Spirit who gives life; the flesh is of no avail. The words that I have spoken to you are spirit and life." The word *life* in these two verses is the Greek word *zoe*. It refers to those who have put on Christ as their Lord and Savior; who have received a blessed life now and eternal life hereafter.[1] So the first benefit of clinging to God's Word is life.

The next benefit and necessity of God's Word is as our washing water. Ephesians 5:25-26 says, "Husbands, love your wives, as Christ loved the church and gave himself up for her, that he might sanctify her, having cleansed her by the washing of water with the word." Jesus Christ cleanses us with His words, as water cleanses our human bodies.

The Bible is also our spiritual food. Matthew 4:4 says, "Man shall not live by bread alone, but by every word that comes from the mouth of God." Job 23:12 says, "I have not departed from the commandment of his lips; I have treasured the words of his mouth more than my portion of food." This phrase, "I have treasured" is the Hebrew word *tsaphan* which means to hide, esteem, store up.[2] Job says he gives more attention to treasuring and storing up God's words than to making sure he has enough food, which is necessary for survival.

Let there be a greater emphasis on storing up God's Word in our heart than on ensuring we have necessary food. First Peter 2:2 says, "Like newborn infants, long for the pure spiritual milk, that by it you may grow up to salvation." The intake of and meditation upon God's Word is vital for our spiritual sustenance, and should be esteemed as such.

And finally, the Word of God is our health and medicine. In Proverbs 4:20-22 we read, "My son, be attentive to my words; incline your ear to my sayings. Let them not escape from your sight; keep them within your heart. For they are life to those who find them, and healing to all their flesh." There is life to be found in the Bible, and the treasure of God's Word is more valuable than healthy flesh. So consider God's Word to be as necessary as health and life.

If your physical body can't exist apart from water, food, health, and even life, how can you be spiritually sustained apart from the Word of God? Apart from knowing God through His Word, there is no other source in all the world that can bring lasting joy. Yet we have access to the words of life, which will impart to us the very joy of Christ, and that joy in its fullness!

FELLOWSHIP BRINGS JOY

The guaranteed and ultimate source of joy is always fellowship with the Lord. But there is also a sweet, hearty joy that results from fellowship with other believers. David said in Psalm 122:1, "I was glad when they said to me, 'Let us go to the house of the LORD!'" It is not enough for us to only worship God by ourselves; we also need to worship God with other believers. We must not "forsake the assembling of ourselves together"

(Hebrews 10:25 KJV). God gives us joy in the company of other believers, as *His presence* makes the fellowship sweet.

We should stir up one another with excitement to come to the house of God. When others invited David to God's house, he rejoiced. He did not despise the invitation to worship God from those who were lower than him. He didn't meditate on their shortcomings or think of ways he may have been wronged by them in the past. Instead, he was glad when they invited him to go up to the house of the Lord.

A necessary sharpening occurs when we are in the company of other Christians. "Iron sharpens iron, and one man sharpens another" (Proverbs 27:17). By our conversations with learned and godly people we become sharper and more profitable. It makes sense, then, that we should be cautious about whom we allow to be our close friends. As much as possible, choose friends who will stir you up and provoke you to love and to good works (Hebrews 10:24).

We have a strong ability to provoke zeal in each other. Peter said, "Therefore I intend always to remind you of these qualities, though you know them and are established in the truth that you have. I think it right, as long as I am in this body, to stir you up by way of reminder" (2 Peter 1:12-13). Our words are very powerful, and we can greatly edify and stir one another up with them. It is important to direct the conversations we have with other saints to edification, and not to vain and empty words. Provoke one another to love and good works.

When we see the faithfulness of God in the lives of others, it can encourage and remind us that God will be faithful in our own lives. The testimonies of those through whom God has worked give us confidence to continue obeying God and seeking to know Him. When we see and hear the answers that God has given to the prayers of His saints, we are motivated to pray with greater fervency ourselves.

Another blessing of fellowship is the opportunity to receive and give exhortation. Just as salt can help food maintain its freshness, so the urging of one another to take action in obeying Christ keeps us from rotting.

Hebrews 3:13 explains this truth, saying, "But exhort one another every day, as long as it is called 'today, that none of you may be hardened by the deceitfulness of sin." Sin is deceitful. The exhortations of our brothers and sisters are a preservative against the hardening and deceitfulness of sin. We need to make every effort to both exhort others and receive exhortation ourselves. The consequences of sin are severe, and God will use the edification of saints to preserve us from sin's deception. Imagine a nine-year-old Twinkie without the preservatives! Without fellowship, we can rot more than a decayed and moldy lunchbox snack.

Believers are necessary in one another's lives. In addition to sharpening, motivating, encouraging, and exhorting one another, great joy results from simply loving each other. The love believers can express to each other greatly exceeds the love that the world understands. We have the love of Christ as our example, and the love we demonstrate to each other should reflect the unfeigned love of Christ to us. First Peter 1:22 says, "Having purified your souls by your obedience to the truth for a sincere brotherly love, love one another earnestly from a pure heart."

The love that we have for one another is also a great witness to the world. Jesus declared, "A new commandment I give to you, that you love one another: just as I have loved you, you also are to love one another. By this all people will know that you are my disciples, if you have love for one another" (John 13:34-35). Because of our love for one another, even those who are blind and dead in sins can discern we're the disciples of Jesus. God has called us to fellowship with one another that we might love one another. All the activities and endeavors involved in fellowshipping with the saints should be motivated by love.

Our love for one another is such a primary and necessary part of our salvation that John says in 1 John 3:14, "We know that we have passed out of death into life, because we love the brothers. Whoever does not love abides in death." If we do not show love to our brethren, than we cannot call ourselves Christians. And just as loving the brethren is a necessary evidence of our salvation, so is keeping the commandments of God necessary to our loving the brethren. "By this we know that we love the children of God, when we love God and obey his commandments" (1 John 5:2).

Not actively loving the saints will rob you of joy. In my life, I've seen women struggling with depression rooted in loneliness, while the loneliness resulted from their not reaching out to others. I have gone through phases in my own life when I've struggled with enthusiastically reaching out to others. I never meant to not reach out to others, I just didn't try hard enough to go out of my way to love others when it meant possible rejection by someone who didn't want my friendship. And the result was that I did have fewer friends and more loneliness.

It's not at all necessary to have a lot of friends to be a godly woman. It is absolutely necessary to love one another with a pure heart fervently if you want to be a godly woman.

If you feel depressed because you are lonely, evaluate how friendly you are. How often do you call or invite those who are not in your "inner circle" to spend time with you? What things have you done this week to reach out to women who may be struggling with loneliness themselves? Do you actively pursue love, and love the women in your life with a pure heart fervently? Search your heart as you answer these questions.

If you actively go out of your way to love, welcome, edify, and bless other women, I want to highly commend you for that. If you have lacked in this area, be encouraged, because it is God who will teach you how to love others. God is the greatest teacher on love there is, and just as He has taught many women before you how to reach out with fervent love and friendliness, He can also teach you.

One thing I often felt very insecure about when I was a younger believer was that I didn't know how to be friendly. During my first semester at Bible college I began to see how reaching out and loving people was not a natural instinct of mine. I longed to obey God and love the believers with pure fervent love, but I didn't even know where to start. I would watch other sisters in Christ be so friendly with each other, and I saw myself as being very cold. I began to pray fervently that I would learn to be friendlier.

It was during one of those times of prayer that I read 1 Thessalonians 4:9. It says, "Now concerning brotherly love you have no need for anyone to write to you, for you yourselves have been taught by God to love one another."

As I read this verse, it leaped off the page at me and buried itself in my heart. God allowed me to see that *He* would instruct me on how to love others. My heart was filled with joyfulness because I realized God Himself would be the one to teach me how to love others, and I would have no greater teacher on earth!

We don't base our love for others on their love for us, but on the love of the Father toward us. He loved us before we ever loved Him. Romans 5:8 says, "But God shows his love for us in that while we were still sinners, Christ died for us." If Christ died for us while we were still separated from Him as His enemies, how much more should we be willing to simply reach out to those who may not receive it?

In Philippians 2:17-18, Paul rejoices that he could give himself for the service of the saints, saying, "Even if I am to be poured out as a drink offering upon the sacrificial offering of your faith, I am glad and rejoice with you all. Likewise you also should be glad and rejoice with me." Being used of God to edify his brethren and glorify Christ was a great reason for him to rejoice. The fellowship we have with believers for the increase of their faith and ours is a great cause of our rejoicing.

Rather than finding your happiness in your own promotion or gain, find happiness in being used by God as a living sacrifice in the advancement of the faith of the saints. Be poured out by God that others might drink of the life of Christ. Go up to the house of God rejoicing at the opportunity you have to minister God's love to others!

~7~

Satisfied With Serving

Do not be anxious about anything, but in everything by prayer and supplication with thanksgiving let your requests be made known to God. And the peace of God, which surpasses all understanding, will guard your hearts and your minds in Christ Jesus.
Philippians 4:6-

Sara hated pain. She shuddered when the doctor described the surgery. Everything the doctor had said about her grandma's health was dismal. Even the chairs in the meeting room were a cold ice blue vinyl.

But she had to hear about the hospital's procedures. She was the only relative qualified to donate a portion of her liver, though it was not her idea of a fun spring break.

Her grandma's warm hand clasped hers thankfully, as the ramifications of the surgery were explained in great detail. Without the operation, her grandma would surely die soon. If the surgery were successful, her grandma could live for many more years. Knowing she could choose to save her grandma's life, Sara signed the consent forms and the date was scheduled.

The procedure went smoothly, and both Sara and her grandma recovered completely. Her grandma's vibrancy returned, and once again they were able to meet together to sip tea and talk about the verses in the Bible they were excited about that day.

One morning, while Sara was sitting cozily on her grandma's dated orange and blue couch, her grandma began to cry. Though they were very close, never had Sara seen her grandma cry like this. She wasn't sure how to react, so she waited for her grandma to speak. She didn't have to wait long.

"Sara, what you did for me—giving me part of your liver—thank you. Your gift to me…" Her voice broke, as she could no longer explain how grateful she was. But Sara knew. She knew her grandma wished she had some way to repay Sara for her sacrifice. But Sara's joy in knowing she was able to serve her grandma was enough.

"Grandma, knowing I was able to do something so precious for you has given me so much elation. I've never felt more satisfied than I did after being able help you in this way."

Sara sat back on the couch. She thought about how she had been more satisfied by serving her grandma than she'd ever been by pursuing things for herself. Helping her grandma had brought her greater joy than any possession or liberty she'd ever attained.

Like Sara, serving others is one of the ways God has given us for happiness. Instead of doing everything we do for ourselves, when we devote ourselves to help others for the glory of God, there will be a great reward.

Being a servant is more than just "how much" time or effort we put into our serving. Washing the dishes and laundry of others is not enough to be happy! Instead, the joy that results from doing things for others is dependant on our heart attitude while serving. Pray that the Lord would reveal your heart motive in all you do, so that every "service" you do for the Lord would be pure and praiseworthy in His sight. Now, let's see what the Bible says about our service to each other and the Lord.

GENEROSITY BRINGS JOY

My husband is naturally very generous. He finds great joy in giving. He loves the Scriptures that talk about the blessings of giving, and he could cheerfully give even his last dollar without a care or regret.

Generosity, especially towards the poor, is something God richly blesses. In Proverbs 19:17 we read that "whoever is generous to the poor lends to the LORD, and he will repay him for his deed." God will reimburse you for what you give to the poor, and He can do it with both money and that which cannot be bought! "Blessed is the one who considers the poor! In the day of trouble the LORD delivers him; the LORD protects him and keeps him alive; he is called blessed in the land; you do not give him up to the will of his enemies. The LORD sustains him on his sickbed; in his illness you restore him to full health" (Psalm 41:1-3).

Those who are considerate to the poor have the promise of God to be delivered in time of trouble, to be preserved and kept alive, to be blessed upon the earth, and to be protected from the desires of their enemies. God also says He will strengthen them on their sickbed and sustain them with His comfort. With such great promises, we might be motivated to give only to receive again. And truly we will receive, and our reward will be from God Himself.

However, though we'll receive blessings from God, He desires us to give our gift for His glory, and not to expect repayment from those to whom we give. In Luke 6:35-38, Jesus explains this saying,

> But love your enemies, and do good, and lend, expecting nothing in return, and your reward will be great, and you will be sons of the Most High, for he is kind to the ungrateful and the evil. Be merciful, even as your Father is merciful. Judge not, and you will not be judged; condemn not, and you will not be condemned; forgive, and you will be forgiven; give, and it will be given to you. Good measure, pressed down, shaken together, running over, will be put into your lap. For with the measure you use it will be measured back to you.

A generous woman will receive generously herself. I know this to be very true from watching my husband receive great things in return for his generosity.

> The point is this: whoever sows sparingly will also reap sparingly, and whoever sows bountifully will also reap bountifully. Each one must give as he has made up his mind, not reluctantly or under compulsion, for God loves a cheerful giver. And God is able to make all grace abound to you, so that having all sufficiency in all things at all times, you may abound in every good work.
> (2 Corinthians 9:6-8)

If we sow what God has given us generously, we'll reap it generously again. The analogy in the above verse with seeds is powerful. Consider what size a farmer's harvest would be if he only planted ten seeds across his fields. Compare this with a farmer who spreads 500,000 seeds on his land. With the same conditions affecting both crops, which farmer would reap a greater harvest? Of course it would be the farmer who sowed more seed.

God declares that those who sow generously will reap generously and those who sow sparingly will reap sparingly. It may seem more profitable to withhold excess money for ourselves, and the Bible is clear that saving is wise (Proverbs 30:24-25), but we must trust that God will reward our generosity, and that in giving we are actually insuring ourselves against poverty. Proverbs 28:27 says, "Whoever gives to the poor will not want, but he who hides his eyes will get many a curse."

Now that we've seen the upside of generosity, let's glance at the downside of stinginess. Proverbs 21:13 says, "Whoever closes his ear to the cry of the poor will himself call out and not be answered." What a fearful place to be, where you know that when you are in need and cry out, no one will hear your cry or care. How much better it is to obey God and give to those in need.

When God commands us to give and be generous, His instructions are accompanied by promises. Our consideration for those in need will cause us to be repaid by God, receive His protection, be blessed on earth, receive rewards in heaven, and reap generously.

If we do not consider the poor, and if we shut our ears to their cries, we will experience many curses and our own cries will not be heard. No wonder the Bible says in Acts 20:35, "In all things I have shown you that by working hard in this way we must help the weak and remember the words of the Lord Jesus, how he himself said, 'It is more blessed to give than to receive.'" Not only do great blessings accompany our generosity, but giving in itself is a blessing to us. Proverbs 22:9 says, "Whoever has a bountiful eye will be blessed, for he shares his bread with the poor."

Another reward that God gives for our kindness to the poor is happiness. Proverbs 14:21 says, "He that despiseth his neighbour sinneth: but he that hath mercy on the poor, happy [is] he" (KJV). Increase your joy by increasing your mercy toward the poor. Jesus explains in the gospel of Luke a practical way to extend kindness to those who do not have much, saying,

> When you give a dinner or a banquet, do not invite your friends or your brothers or your relatives or rich neighbors, lest they also invite you in return and you be repaid. But when you give a feast, invite the poor, the crippled, the lame, the blind, and you will be blessed, because they cannot repay you. You will be repaid at the resurrection of the just.
>
> (Luke 14:12-14)

God will reward our compassion when we are resurrected into glory, and those rewards are eternal. Hebrews 6:10 says, "For God is not so unjust as to overlook your work and the love that you showed for his sake in serving the saints, as you still do." The rewards that we receive in heaven will never fade away or be stolen. Even if we forget those things that we do in generosity, God won't forget.

What, then, should be our priority concerning generosity? "So then, as we have opportunity, let us do good to everyone, and especially to those who are of the household of faith" (Galatians 6:10). Let us especially do good unto our brothers and sisters in the Lord, knowing Christ has first given to us everything we give to others. "For you know the grace of our Lord Jesus Christ, that though he was rich, yet for your sake he became poor, so that you by his poverty might become rich" (2 Corinthians 8:9). If our Lord Jesus Christ, who is God of all, became poor for our sake, how much more should we be willing to sacrifice some earthly pleasure to do good unto others?

With this in mind, let's seek the Lord earnestly about the measure we sow, because God rewards the happy giver *with even more happiness!*

PRAYER BRINGS JOY

In this section I want us to overview the subject of prayer; including intercessory prayer that serves others, prayer that worships God, and prayer for our own personal needs and longings. All three types are for our joy.

Intercessory prayer is a way to serve others. It can be one of the most beautiful labors of love any Christian can do for someone else. It is spending time praying for the needs and burdens of others with the same or greater fervency that we pray for our own needs. When we intercede for another person, we are bearing their burdens. By spending our time lifting up another person's needs before God, we are serving them immeasurably.

Prayer also includes honoring and adoring God. Just thinking about what prayer is brings me joy! Prayer is the sublime privilege of being able to talk to God. The high priest who ministered before the Lord one day a year had to fear for his life when entering the holiest place of the temple behind the veil. Because he could only come into God's presence if the right sacrifices had been made, the high priest risked death in that holiest place (Exodus 28:35, Leviticus 16:2).

In the book of Esther in the Old Testament, Esther the queen had to fear for her life when entering the throne room of her husband the king—for if he did not raise his scepter when she entered, she would be killed! (Esther 4:16).

What is amazing is the crucial difference between the approach of Esther to the king, the high priest to the holiest of all, and our approach now to God. Esther and the high priest feared death, but we've been instructed by the God of love to come boldly before His throne: "Let us then with confidence draw near to the throne of grace, that we may receive mercy and find grace to help in time of need" (Hebrews 4:16).

When we enter the throne room of the Most High God in prayer, we don't have to fear for our lives, but we can come boldly in full assurance of faith! Just as Esther was accepted by her husband the king, God has raised His scepter for us to approach His presence.

And that scepter was raised as Jesus was lifted up before all men on the cross. As pain ripped through His body, Jesus cried out His final words from the cross, "It is finished" and willingly breathed His last (John 19:30).

Suddenly, the thick veil in the temple was ripped from top to bottom (Matthew 27:51). I can only imagine the shock and horror on the faces of the people in the temple at that moment when, there in front of them, the sacred and private holiest of all was abruptly exposed. The two gold cherubim and mercy seat were revealed to the whole temple.

To understand how significant this event was, read the previous instructions that God had given to Moses about this Most Holy Place: "Tell Aaron your brother not to come at any time into the Holy Place inside the veil, before the mercy seat that is on the ark, *so that he may not die*. For I will appear in the cloud over the mercy seat" (Leviticus 16:2, italics added). Behind the veil was the dwelling place of God! To come into that place meant death, and now God had ripped the veil.

The physical veil was ripped to demonstrate something even more significant. The barrier between God and man was removed in Christ's flesh (Hebrews 10:20). Through the crucifixion of Jesus the Messiah, the way has been prepared for us to approach the throne of God and enter in boldly. What a holy privilege! The all-powerful, holy, King of all kings allows us free access into His presence.

No one and no thing can compare to our God's majesty and power, and yet, in the magnitude of His greatness, how blessed we are that He considers us! And as our God is good though He is great, so Esther also approached a king who considered her request. Though she might have perished, instead she was told she could receive whatever she would ask, even up to half the kingdom!

Esther's husband was willing to do for her much more than her request. Know that often God is willing to do for us much more than we request. The grace of God incomparably exceeds all the kindnesses of men, and we have the promise of God that if we ask, we shall receive (Matthew 7:7). Esther came in fear, but we can come in confidence. We have God's assurance that He wants us to come, and we have the promise of His answer. Esther had to approach the king alone, but we enter His presence with an advocate, Jesus Christ the righteous (1 John 2:1).

So, with both our understanding of His love for us, and our reverence of Him, we approach Him to pray. Because even though we are to have boldness in approaching God, He is still to be revered, as the God who holds our very breath in His hands!

When the apostles approached God's presence in prayer they said, "Sovereign Lord, who made the heaven and the earth and the sea and everything in them" (Acts 4:24). They began their prayer and supplication to God by acknowledging He'd created all things! We need to understand our place before God, and pray to Him with godly fear and reverence.

The presence of those who occupy the places of highest importance can be fear-provoking, and how much more should we fear the presence of the living God. We don't fear Him as if He will be cruel to us, because we know that the Bible has promised and assured us that His thoughts toward us are for good and not for evil, but we fear Him because of who He is. If your closest friend were the Queen of her country, you would respect her for her position but understand that she still loved you as her friend. We fear God because He is God, but understand that toward us He is kind and gentle and only judges righteous judgment.

When we approach God in prayer, we must maintain only the very highest respect and honor of Him, yet still trust Him completely with our lives and cast even our very smallest and silliest care upon Him, because He cares for us. Prayer is not voluntary, but we are commanded to pray always. And this is for our good—because God desires us to be people who are glad and who always rejoice. Jesus says that through prayer, and through God answering our prayers, we will have fullness of joy.

In John 16:23-24, Jesus says that if we ask the Father our requests in His name, He will give us what we have asked: "In that day you will ask nothing of me. Truly, truly, I say to you, whatever you ask of the Father in my name, he will give it to you. Until now you have asked nothing in my name. Ask, and you will receive, that your joy may be full."

Let me tell you about a time when I had tremendous joy from receiving the request I had asked from the Lord. Some years ago, before I was married, our church was planning a vision tour to India, and I very much wanted to be a part of the trip. However, the cost for the trip was out of my league, and there was no way I would be able to go unless the Lord provided the money for me. I was praying for weeks I would be able to go. As the deadline for purchasing airplane tickets approached, I prayed more and more fervently.

On the final morning, when the tickets were being purchased, I still had no way of going on my own. I paced the house praying for the Lord to provide if it was His will for me to go on the trip, and I waited. I was waiting for a phone call from my friend who would let me know if there was enough money gathered from our church in sponsorships. Finally the phone rang, and she told me I was going.

I was thrilled, but it wasn't until I hung up the phone that I went running through the house jumping and praising God. My joy was completely full at that moment, as I had both asked and received of the Lord. I felt so in awe of God because of His provision for me, and that awe resulted in joy that was complete in every particular.

If you want to experience fullness of joy, ask God your requests in the name of Jesus and expect to receive. Don't miss out on the gladness available to you through answered prayer.

OBEDIENCE AS A SERVANT TO THE LORD BRINGS JOY

Promoting yourself, for your own honor and admiration, is the sure course to eventual misery. Seeking any glory or promotion for yourself apart from the glory of God is pride. But when you humble yourself under the mighty hand of God, He will exalt you in due time (1 Peter 5:6). The call to walk with God is the call to put your hand to the plow and not look back. Jesus said in Luke 9:62, "No one who puts his hand to the plow and looks back is fit for the kingdom of God."

Being a Christian means committing to count all things loss to know Christ. It's the willingness to relinquish everything you consider dear, if God were to ask it of you. It's the continual giving of yourself to God without reserve and without thought of your own glory. The call to follow Christ is the call to pick up your cross and follow Him, even as He carried His cross to His death.

When we take upon ourselves the mindset that counts all things loss, there becomes nothing too lowly or too humbling for us to involve ourselves in, apart from sin. Taking up our cross daily to follow Christ is the only lifestyle God has declared acceptable. Jesus said, "If anyone would come after me, let him deny himself and take up his cross daily and follow me" (Luke 9:23). Desire as we might, God has declared that there is no other way to follow Him than to do it wholeheartedly, with a complete denial of ourselves.

When we choose to follow Christ, and believe in Him, there can no longer be a place for self-seeking, self-promotion, or even the phrase "I deserve." According to the Bible, we deserve only to be punished eternally for our sin in a completely black, painful, burning lake of fire. It is by God's own grace alone we have been redeemed from that future torment, and He requires that we count all other things loss and obey Him completely.

With this in mind, there can be no true calling of God or commandment by Him that is acceptable to resist. This includes preaching the gospel, obeying the laws of the country, submission to our own husbands in everything, and not seeking the praise of man, but only the praise of God. We know what is required of us, because God has given us His Word, which plainly declares His will for us. Part of being a servant is humbling yourself and submitting to another person in obedience, whether it be to your husband, your parents, the government, or any other authority. Stooping low to humble yourself and take the road of an obedient servant before God is what will ultimately bring greater joy.

If you have the mindset that says, "I'm not going to let my husband tell me what to do, because I'm stronger than that," then you're actually weak. It's easy and in agreement with our sinful nature to resist authority and seek out what we want. A truly strong woman is the one who voluntarily places herself in subjection to another person if it's in accordance with the Bible. It's much harder for a woman to humble herself and surrender her will than to seek her own will.

Another aspect of serving is being willing to help people and to care for them. For instance, let's say my sister needed my help on a day I had planned to reorganize my closet. If I were to say—"I'm not going to help my sister out and pick her up from the mechanic because it won't be convenient for me. She could have taken care of this earlier and she has lots of other friends who could help her."—I would not be making any sacrifice to serve her. I would likely be demonstrating that I consider myself as more important than her. My decision would ultimately reveal my selfish priorities and my lack of desire to give of myself sacrificially. Now I don't believe we are obligated to say "yes" to every need. It's important for us to make wise choices concerning how we spend our time, but we are also called to serve others, even when it may be inconvenient and cost us something.

But doing what honors God at all costs is what will ultimately satisfy us and please God. Jesus only did what pleased the Father, even when it meant being hurt, shamed, being made fun of, and killed. Consider the example we have of Jesus, who was God of all, and yet voluntarily humbled Himself to be obedient to His Father.

In John 13, we read the striking story about Jesus washing His disciples' feet. As the Passover feast was ending, Jesus rose from supper and girded Himself with a towel. After pouring water into a basin, He began to wash each of His disciples' feet and then to wipe them with the towel He was wearing.

This act Jesus did for His disciples was a job usually reserved for the lowest servants. Yet, according to verse 3, Jesus was the farthest thing on earth from the stature of a lowly servant: He knew "that the Father had given all things into his hands, and that he was come from God, and went to God." He knew who He was as God, and that the Father had given Him all authority. Jesus washed His disciples' feet to give them an example, even though He knew that He'd come from God.

Through His example we learn there is nothing too humbling for us to do in obedience to God, because "Truly, truly, I say to you, a servant is not greater than his master, nor is a messenger greater than the one who sent him" (John 13:16). We should serve others willingly, even if it means we must humble ourselves, because we are in no way greater than our Lord Jesus. And as we are obedient to the Lord as a servant, Jesus says the result will be happiness. John 13:17 says, "If ye know these things, happy are ye if ye do them" (KJV).

Jesus knew the Father had given all things into His hands. Understanding from what high level of honor and stature Jesus humbled Himself is crucial to really understanding how great His example is. Jesus said of Himself in Matthew 11:27, "All things have been handed over to me by my Father." Again in John 3:35 Jesus said, "The Father loves the Son and has given all things into his hand." There is nothing that God the Father has held back from Jesus the Son. Even in His humanity, while on earth during His first coming, Jesus said that God the Father had given Him all things. He had authority over everything, with the assurance He would also one day be judge of all humankind.

In John 5:22-23 Jesus said, "The Father judges no one, but has given all judgment to the Son, that all may honor the Son, just as they honor the Father. Whoever does not honor the Son does not honor the Father who sent him." Imagine knowing that in ten years you would be the richest person in the world. Would that change how you acted now? Jesus knew while He walked on this earth in frail human flesh that He would be the one judging and condemning those same people who mocked Him in unbelief. Jesus was aware of who He was, and that He was God, even while He suffered the despicable shame of crucifixion.

He also knew He had "authority over all flesh, to give eternal life to all whom [the Father had] given him" (John 17:2). Another truth Jesus knew about Himself was He had the power to reveal God the Father to anyone He wanted: "All things have been handed over to me by my Father, and no one knows who the Son is except the Father, or who the Father is except the Son and anyone to whom the Son chooses to reveal him" (Luke 10:22). The Son had the authority to reveal who the Father was to whomever He wanted, and He still willingly washed His disciples' feet.

God, who *spoke* the world into existence, humbled Himself by becoming a man. And He chose to humble Himself even further by doing the lowliest job of a servant, and then finally experiencing the degrading shame of dying a public and excruciating death on a cross.

This is the one whom we serve, and a servant is not greater than his Lord. So do not think it strange that we also are called to give of ourselves humbly and with a great sacrifice. Find joy in obedience, in serving, and in humility, because the only way to know Christ better in His obedience, serving, and humility is by experiencing those things yourself. And remember how He spoke the words, "If ye know these things, happy are ye if ye do them" (John 13:17 KJV).

~8~

From the Mouth

Walk in a manner worthy of the Lord, fully pleasing to him, bearing fruit in every good work and increasing in the knowledge of God. May you be strengthened with all power, according to his glorious might, for all endurance and patience with joy, giving thanks to the Father, who has qualified you to share in the inheritance of the saints in light.
Colossians 1:10-12

My children were growing restless. We were still over an hour away from our destination, and I was sure my young daughter would start crying at any moment. As we drove up the "grapevine," a very bare stretch of road on the 5 Freeway leading up through the state of California, my eyes glazed over at the sight of the same familiar hills I had seen on this repetitious drive. I had already passed the last useful exit for a good twenty miles.

At that moment, cars began to slow down suddenly, until we were all at a standstill on the road. With nowhere to go and nothing to do, we waited. After about ten minutes of being completely stopped, people began to walk up and down the lanes of cars. Next to us was a trailer, and soon they had propped up the side opening and set up camp.

On top of all this, it was a boiling hot day. How thankful I was that, with two kids in the car, I had a tank full of gas and I could run the air-conditioning. As people mingled around, I quickly found out that a huge fire was approaching the freeway about a mile or so up ahead, so all traffic had been stopped until the fire could be contained. Someone had allowed a cigarette to fly out their window, and that small, insignificant little burning object had ignited a huge fire.

Airplanes began to fly over the hills less than a few hundred yards away and smoke assaulted the air. I prayed for protection and tried my best to entertain the kids. In less than an hour, the freeway started moving again and we were free. The fire was still blazing, but it was safely away from the road.

Remembering this incident brings James 3:5-6 to my mind: "So also the tongue is a small member, yet it boasts of great things. How great a forest is set ablaze by such a small fire!" Such a small object had cause such a great fire. Our tongues are small compared to the size of our bodies, yet they direct the courses of our lives.

By the tongue, women gain and lose friends; presidents are elected to office; conspiracies are plotted. The power of the tongue is staggering. It can be used to curse God or bless men (James 3:9). The tongue can push men closer to the fires of hell and it can set men ablaze with passion for God. And each of us has been given one of these powerful tongues.

Not only can the tongue cause us harm, but it can bring us unlimited happiness. Use your words to glorify God and watch the joy that is produced by the small muscle called the tongue.

WHAT WE SPEAK CAN BRING JOY

The Proverbs say that "to make an apt answer is a joy to a man, and a word in season, how good it is!" (Proverbs 15:23). We can bring joy to ourselves just by speaking the right things. Proverbs 16:24 says, "Gracious words are like a honeycomb, sweetness to the soul and health to the body."

There are great benefits to those who speak right things with their mouth: joy, sweetness of soul, health, and even justification. Jesus said in Matthew 12:37, "For by your words you will be justified, and by your words you will be condemned."

Speaking the right words is a great source of joy and good for those who possess wisdom. Proverbs 12:14 says, "From the fruit of his mouth a man is satisfied with good." Speak right, edifying, godly things and you will bring delight to yourself and others. Proverbs 16:13 says, "Righteous lips are the delight of a king, and he loves him who speaks what is right."

If you struggle with depression, evaluate what kinds of things you talk about. What subjects do your conversations center on? Do you complain or give thanks? Do you worry out loud or remind others of God's faithfulness? Do you talk about your weight or the weight of God's glory? What you talk about with others will have a big influence on how happy you are.

Ephesians 4:29 gives a brilliant definition of what speaking right things consists of: "Let no corrupting talk come out of your mouths, but only such as is good for building up, as fits the occasion, that it may give grace to those who hear." We are called to not speak anything that is corrupt, at all. Rather, we are to speak what is good, and those things that edify others and minister grace to our listeners. When you speak things you know are right and please God, rejoice and continue to let your mouth be a source of happiness to you.

ENCOURAGING OTHERS BRINGS JOY

Encouragement is truly comforting. Being recognized for something that has blessed others, when God is ultimately being given the glory, can be very refreshing. I'm also encouraged when I'm reminded of God's character; that He is good, faithful, and sovereign. First Thessalonians 5:11 says, "Encourage one another and build one another up, just as you are doing." It's vitally important that we're diligent to exhort and comfort one another.

Do you know anyone who needs to be reminded that God is still faithful even though things are difficult? Have you ever needed a reminder like that yourself? Do you ever want to be reassured that you are cared about and loved? When people feel lonely, unimportant, or not accepted by others, even a simple and genuine hug can be very encouraging.

When I feel lonely, I try to ask myself, "How many people have I reached out to today?" If you ever feel lonesome, ask yourself if you've gone out of your way that day to be friendly with those who aren't just your close friends. So often when we feel lonely, it's because we haven't taken the initiative to reach out to other people who may also be lonely.

There's no temptation that's not common to man, and so if you're tempted to feel "left out," other people are also experiencing the same emotions as you. Observe the women in your church and around you who are not being crowded by people and reach out to them. This is such a blessed cure to feeling left out.

Sometimes loneliness seeps in because a woman feels like her friends don't really like her or that they are secretly annoyed by her. I've had women tell me they feel unliked, when I know they are very well-liked. Maybe you feel as if you're that member of the body who is ignored.

In these times it's crucial we focus on what's most important. Is your goal in life to be well-liked by people or pleasing to God? If you're seeking popularity, you're only setting yourself up for disappointment when someone is more admired than you. Our security can't come from people or it will be shaken during every storm.

If our confidence is based on being liked or praised, our emotions will be dependant on people and we won't be serving Christ. Galatians 1:10 says, "For am I now seeking the approval of man, or of God? Or am I trying to please man? If I were still trying to please man, I would not be a servant of Christ." A woman whose security rests on God won't be overly upset when people reject her; instead she'll be confident the Father

Himself loves her (John 16:27). She will believe that God has accepted her.

Precious sister, God has accepted you. The Bible says you are accepted in the beloved: "To the praise of the glory of his grace, wherein he hath made us accepted in the beloved" (Ephesians 1:6 KJV). You are vitally necessary to the body. God has made you accepted in the beloved because He loves you. John 16:27 says, "For the Father himself loves you, because you have loved me and have believed that I came from God." Be confident in God's love for you. It will make you able to minister more effectively to the needs of others, because your own needs will be met.

If you pursue friendships with wise women, you will grow in wisdom also. But do not be partial in your friendships because of any exterior quality or characteristic. James 2:1 commands us to not show partiality, saying, "My brothers, show no partiality as you hold the faith in our Lord Jesus Christ, the Lord of glory." If you only are seeking to reach out to those people who are wealthy, beautiful, or well-liked, then you have become a "judge with evil thoughts" (James 2:4). James again reiterates this point, saying, "But if you show partiality, you are committing sin and are convicted by the law as transgressors" (James 2:9). When you differentiate in your love to people because of partiality, you commit sin. God is not pleased with anything less in your love toward the saints than to "love one another with a pure heart fervently" (1 Peter 1:22 KJV).

Be careful as you read this to not think about those people who've shown partiality to you. Instead think about if you've avoided people yourself. I'm not saying to develop close friendships with just anybody, because a wise woman will be discerning about her close friends, but we can maintain a distance with people while still loving them fervently.

The Bible says that all believers, regardless of their stature, their position in the church, their past, their trials, their financial status, their level of need, regardless of anything and everything; every believer is absolutely necessary to the body. "The parts of the body that seem to be weaker are indispensable" (1 Corinthians 12:22).

With this in mind, encourage one another. Think of someone you can encourage with the truth of Scripture and go do it. And in encouraging one another, and being edified by one another, rejoice!

PREACHING THE GOSPEL BRINGS JOY

God has given us the ministry of reconciliation. Since we have enjoyed the great blessing of our own reconciliation with God, He now asks us to share the Word of reconciliation with others. Second Corinthians 5:18-22 says,

> All this is from God, who through Christ reconciled us to himself and gave us the ministry of reconciliation; that is, in Christ God was reconciling the world to himself, not counting their trespasses against them, and entrusting to us the message of reconciliation. Therefore, we are ambassadors for Christ, God making his appeal through us. We implore you on behalf of Christ, be reconciled to God. For our sake he made him to be sin who knew no sin, so that in him we might become the righteousness of God.

When we are obedient to God in pleading with others to be reconciled to Him, there is a great opportunity for joy.

About a month ago, I went into a small vitamin shop I hadn't been to before. The salesgirl and I had talked about different things, and during our conversation I asked her if she'd heard of the Ten Commandments. She hadn't, so I asked her about her religious background. She told me that she grew up as a Hindu. I left her with a few different tracts that I had in my purse, and found out her name so I could begin praying for her.

Today I ran out of the product that I had bought from her store, so I went back to buy more. Having already established a rapport with her, I felt strongly that I needed to explain what the gospel was. I excitedly entered the store, and my excitement wasn't over what I was planning to buy. I knew that God had called me to explain Jesus to her, but while I was in the store it got very crowded. We talked briefly, but she was busy so I left. After finishing my shopping in a nearby store, I still felt compelled to go back and talk to her.

This time the store was empty, and my heart began to speed up as I walked through the empty store, past walls covered with glass bottles and small boxes, and toward the back where she was. Since I had no reason except the gospel to come back to the store, I shared with her that God wanted her to be reconciled with Him, and that He was pleading with her through me. I began to share with her the Ten Commandments, so she could see her sin and her need for a Savior.

Then suddenly, as I was talking about the perfection of Christ, and His death and resurrection, my pulse began to race frantically. I cannot remember another time in my life when I have been so nervous. It was strange too, because I was talking only to her, and she was so nice; and there have many other times when I have shared the gospel to much larger groups without any nervousness. Then, because of my racing heart, I forgot where I was going with what I was saying.

I share this so you know the ministry of reconciliation isn't always easy, but it's always necessary. We talked back and forth and I was eventually able to get the whole gospel out even with my shortness of breath. For that I am thankful. I am also blessed that even human blunders can be used by God for His glory. I am reminded of 1 Corinthians 1:26-29, which says,

> For consider your calling, brothers: not many of you were wise according to worldly standards, not many were powerful, not many were of noble birth. But God chose what is foolish in the world to shame the wise; God chose what is weak in the world to shame the strong; God chose what is low and despised in the world, even things that are not, to bring to nothing things that are, so that no human being might boast in the presence of God.

Part of the excitement of preaching Jesus is realizing that many people are learning for the first time they can be saved apart from their works. It is through our sharing with people that they learn God will freely impute the righteousness of Christ to them if they'll come to Him by faith in Jesus.

The store stayed empty the whole time I talked to her, and during the time I was sharing about Jesus, she said she knew God had brought me into her life. When I got in my car I praised God for the utterance He gave me to open my mouth and share, even if it was with "stammering lips" (Isaiah 28:11).

I love sharing the truth of Christ for several reasons. First, people who are alienated from God receive the knowledge they need to be reconciled to Him. Second, preaching the gospel enhances all areas of our Christian walk. Third, there is joy in being obedient to God, because the righteous are bold as a lion (Proverbs 28:1). And fourth, there is the blessed possibility that the lost will become reunited with their God and Savior.

I believe true Christians are called to share the gospel of Christ with unbelievers, and that this is a necessary part of the Christian life. Not having the "gift" of evangelism is not an excuse for not sharing Christ. Praying for utterance is something I think is good for Christians to do for themselves and others daily. Jesus said, "So everyone who acknowledges me before men, I also will acknowledge before my Father who is in heaven, but whoever denies me before men, I also will deny before my Father who is in heaven. Do not think that I have come to bring peace to the earth. I have not come to bring peace, but a sword" (Matthew 10:32-34).

The gospel of life to believers is the stench of death to the unsaved, and there will be people who are very offended at it. There is no sword or stench of death when the unsaved think you are one of them. If Christians appear to be like moral unbelievers, and never speak the truth in love, it's unlikely they will offend very many people. But it's the high calling and responsibility of those who have received remission of sins to share the truth with those who are perishing, even at the cost of offending them. How can anyone hear the gospel without a preacher?

One of the most frustrating sayings to me is: "Preach the gospel. Use words if necessary." The Bible never says this! Live holy lives and use words, because they are necessary! Communicating the gospel is not always fun or easy, but it's always rewarding. Whether we share Christ with fear, trembling, weakness, or all three (1 Corinthians 2:1-5), we must still share Him.

Paul said in 1 Corinthians 9:16-17, "For if I preach the gospel, that gives me no ground for boasting. For necessity is laid upon me. Woe to me if I do not preach the gospel! For if I do this of my own will, I have a reward, but not of my own will, I am still entrusted with a stewardship." Jeremiah said, "If I say, 'I will not mention him, or speak any more in his name,' there is in my heart as it were a burning fire shut up in my bones, and I am weary with holding it in, and I cannot" (Jeremiah 20:9). In Acts 4:20 Peter and John said concerning the gospel: "For we cannot but speak of what we have seen and heard."

The same commandment given to Peter and John has also been given to us. Jesus said, "Go into all the world and proclaim the gospel to the whole creation" (Mark 16:15). James 4:17 says, "So whoever knows the right thing to do and fails to do it, for him it is sin." It is imperative that we're filled with God's Holy Spirit continually so we can be ready to share Christ with others as we're led.

One of my greatest experiences of joy inexpressible and full of glory was when I was filled with the Holy Spirit, and I was boldly preaching the gospel to a group of people in a parking lot and being persecuted (verbally) for it. Often, preaching the gospel is cause for exhilarating happiness.

And if those times for me were glorious, think of the joy Stephen must have experienced in Acts 7 when he saw Jesus as he was being stoned to death. In Acts 6 we read about how a counsel of people were brought together to falsely accuse Stephen. He begins to preach the gospel of Christ, beginning with Abraham, and as he talks the council was filled with anger. Acts 7:54 says, "Now when they heard these things they were enraged, and they ground their teeth at him."

Yet Stephen, "full of the Holy Spirit, gazed into heaven and saw the glory of God, and Jesus standing at the right hand of God. And he said, "Behold, I see the heavens opened, and the Son of Man standing at the right hand of God" (Acts 7:55-56). The people were furious when they heard this, and ran at him with one accord. Then they cast him out of the city and stoned him. Acts 7:59-60 says, "And as they were stoning Stephen, he called out, 'Lord Jesus, receive my spirit.' And falling to his knees he cried out with a loud voice, 'Lord, do not hold this sin against them.' And when he had said this, he fell asleep."

Those who have tasted the joy of God's glory in the face of persecution might be able to comprehend the magnitude of awe Stephen probably felt while dying. The Bible does not say whether he felt the pain of the stoning or not, but we know he only spoke things that were pleasing to God even in his murderous death.

If you want to experience great indescribable joy, go out to preach Christ with other believers in the power of the Holy Spirit. The joy I've experienced while sharing Christ in a witnessing situation, and the joy of Paul and Silas when they sang praises to God after being imprisoned (Acts 16:25) for preaching the gospel—this is a joy that only comes by the Holy Spirit.

Even in times of strong persecution, God will meet us with gladness. First Peter 4:14 says, "If you are insulted for the name of Christ, you are blessed, because the Spirit of glory and of God rests upon you." An indescribable happiness accompanies persecution. Jesus said we are blessed when men come against us to treat us wickedly for His name's sake: "Blessed are you when others revile you and persecute you and utter all kinds of evil against you falsely on my account. Rejoice and be glad, for your reward is great in heaven, for so they persecuted the prophets who were before you" (Matthew 5:11-12).

If we are depending on the strength of Christ to communicate the good news of salvation, relying entirely on Him, and being filled with the Holy Spirit, how can we not help but rejoice? The exceeding gladness that accompanies maltreatment for the gospel's sake is strangely too wonderful for words. When I was being persecuted for Christ's sake I didn't have to try to rejoice. I was overcome with gladness. And that gladness arose in my heart apart from me even thinking about it, because it was the overpouring of the Holy Spirit filling my heart. There is nothing on earth like it!

If possible, make friends with people who share their faith in Christ with others. Being around Christians who love to talk about the gospel to the lost is such a good way to be encouraged to share with the lost yourself.

I also want to mention that sometimes a strong sorrow can accompany rejection for the gospel's sake. The Scriptures have many comforting words when this happens. Jesus said,

> If the world hates you, know that it has hated me before it hated you. If you were of the world, the world would love you as its own; but because you are not of the world, but I chose you out of the world, therefore the world hates you. Remember the word that I said to you: 'A servant is not greater than his master.' If they persecuted me, they will also persecute you. If they kept my word, they will also keep yours.
>
> (John 15:18-20)

While rejoicing in our persecution, we will still sorrow for those who reject Christ. Paul said in Romans 9:2-3 that he had "great sorrow and unceasing anguish in [his] heart" because the majority of Israel had not acknowledged Christ as their Savior. He went on, saying, "For I could wish that I myself were accursed and cut off from Christ for the sake of my brothers, my kinsmen according to the flesh." It's natural for the Christian to sorrow over those who won't repent. Psalm 119:136 says, "My eyes shed streams of tears, because people do not keep your law."

This is one of those great paradoxes of both sorrowing and rejoicing together. We rejoice because "God's firm foundation stands, bearing this seal: 'The Lord knows those who are his'" (2 Timothy 2:19). Yet it's natural for us to feel sorrow when our loved ones or those to whom we minister refuse Christ.

Notwithstanding, God knows those who are His, and there is so much comfort in that when someone rejects the gospel. We also know that sometimes we are sowing or watering a seed, and God will bring the increase even if we never hear about it. So for us, it is better to glorify God by trusting Him than to ever question His ways.

Now here is something else that is very interesting. We can even rejoice when the gospel is preached by others who preach it in themselves, apart from the Holy Spirit, and instead are filled with envy and strife. Why? Because the Bible says to. Philippians 1:18 says, "Only that in every way, whether in pretense or in truth, Christ is proclaimed, and in that I rejoice. Yes, and I will rejoice." Even when the Bible is preached in pretense, and those who do it desire their own glory, we can still rejoice that Christ is preached.

~9~

Training the Emotions

And we know that for those who love God all things work together for good, for those who are called according to his purpose.
Romans 8:28

Training our emotions is the mental "weight-lifting" of our thoughts and feelings to bring glory to God in all things. The issues we're going to be looking at next all deal with the heart and mind; they are primarily inward in their focus, although they are ultimately upward in their focus toward God. These spiritual, internal, and unseen mental toils equip us with a greater ability to fight the war of our tumultuous emotions.

Imagine a soldier: he's standing in a battle zone and beaming with excitement even though the enemy army is charging toward him with their tanks. His mind is so at rest that an onlooker might even be disturbed by his flippant disposition. But a little trip over the hill behind the soldier would reveal what makes this seemingly endangered man so calm; a small bomb has just been accurately fired that will destroy the enemy's army forces and keep his life safely preserved. He knows the bomb is on its way, so the soldier relaxes knowing everything is really under control, and *his side* is winning.

Spiritual labors often remind us that we are on the winning side. God will be the ultimate victor and everything is working for our good, no matter how it may seem in our temporal circumstances.

Give yourself wholeheartedly to spiritual fitness. If it takes someone who is physically fit to win a marathon, it surely takes someone who is spiritually healthy to effectively climb the Everest of emotional control. But at the top, when your heart can gaze without wavering into the glory of pleasing God, and rejoice at His goodness in every jagged hardship of life, the scenery is breathtaking. It's a beautiful view for those whose gaze is fixed on God.

HOPING IN THE LORD BRINGS JOY

Sometimes there are days when we must work at having joy. There are times when the sky is overcast; and when everything looks dreary, we can begin to feel dreary, too. David said, "Why are you cast down, O my soul, and why are you in turmoil within me? Hope in God" (Psalm 42:11). Why do we allow ourselves to be downcast? What causes us to fret? We have a good, merciful, powerful, and wise God to hope in.

Can you see how this might compare to a man who sits in his small apartment, starving because he refuses to buy food and freezing because he refuses to run the heater, all while secretly hoarding billions of dollars in the bank? When we feel hopeless, we become like this foolish man, who had all he needed to be warmed and fed, but refused to access any of the treasures available to him. It is necessary for us to have hope in God if we are going to be consistently and truly joyful.

Depression and suicide are so often the end result of people "having no hope and without God in the world" (Ephesians 2:12). If your life seems like it should be good, and yet you still have a pervading sadness, consider where your hope lies. If your hope is not in God alone, do not be surprised if you feel emotionally depressed. When a woman's focus wanders, her joy will also meander slyly away.

It may seem like a woman's hope is in God, when it may really be that her hope is in God *changing her circumstances.* Women must be careful that their hope in God is in God alone, and not what God might do for them, to please themselves. I love how David said, "And now, O Lord, for what do I wait? My hope is in you" (Psalm 39:7). I usually remind myself of this verse after something disappointing happens; after having put my hope in something other than the Lord, and being failed by it (like I should have known would happen). Only the Lord is always faithful. Hope in Him is the only hope guaranteed to never put us to shame.

What then are we hoping for? We are hoping for the day we see Christ and are made like Him. We are hoping in His Word. We hope in God's mercy and compassion. Our hope is that we may know Jesus more, that we may be transformed into His image, and that God, above all things, would be glorified. This hope will bring us joy, as we "rejoice in hope of the glory of God" (Romans 5:2).

Our hope in God is in contrast to those who have no hope; because they have no stable, true hope. A hope that's secured by the truth of God's Word will not be disappointed. Hope that's hanging on to external conditions is like holding on to the back of a moving car. For some crazy reason, when I was about twelve years old I held on to the bumper of a car driving around a parking lot while my legs trailed behind me on the asphalt. After the pain became too intense, I was forced to let go, and I still have the scars on my knee as evidence.

The penalties of a woman who clings to earthly desires are much more painful than a scraped knee. Desires for treatments that God has not prescribed for us will lead to great injury. What can seem to be only a subtle tug in our hearts for some flirtatious pursuit can have the power to pull us head deep into sin.

And when we're lying face down in the mire, trapped under the burden of what we crave, you'd think we might abandon all our vain desires. But usually, as we suffocate under the weight of fleeting lures, we can't even see what's trapping us. Instead of noticing that we're ensnared by what we want, we sadly think we're trapped by what *keeps us* from getting what we want.

But our earthly desires are more suffocating than anything that stops us from having those desires fulfilled. Women aren't stifled by their lack of time, their lack of money, their lack of a perfect figure, or their lack of a perfect mate; women are stifled by their lack of desire for God!

When longings not based on "things above" (Colossians 3:2) take up space in a heart that should be reserved only for the passionate yearning for God, the woman in whom that heart dwells will feel in some way frustrated. That cloud of other pursuits will block the light of God's joy in some way, forcing gloom in an area of her emotions, and then it's no wonder there will be shadows of depression.

Her ray of hope is found in returning her desires to the peddler who pushed them, without looking for a refund, so she can escape as quickly as possible from the harmful effects. Just as a plant would die without light, we also will die if we're blocked from the light of God's joyous presence. The fleeting longings of this life slaughter the soul that pursues them. Let me share with you what can happen when our hope is in something besides the Lord.

Julianna was thrilled on the day she moved into her new house on the beach. In only eight years, her husband had become the CFO of a large company, and he was now earning a tremendous salary. She loved being able to go shopping for the finest things, and she was very confident that with all the money they were making, all would be well with them and their children. Immersing herself in the culture of her new town, she quickly became accepted among the elite. Her husband also enjoyed their new life, and they maintained a perfect image.

They were invited to the most prestigious parties, and both Julianna and her husband thought life couldn't get better. But, after a time, the light drinking that Julianna had been doing at the parties became a full-fledged addiction. Because of the obsession they had with appearances, it wasn't long before her husband was involved with pornography. She became so involved in her partying that she didn't even notice the affair he began having.

Divorce was the natural next step, and it forced the sale of her house. Her daughter began drinking secretly, and soon her son was dealing drugs. What seemed like an innocent desire to be beautiful, wealthy, and glamorous spiraled into a destructive chasm she could not escape. When the plans she had made were fulfilled, she was left with ruins for a family and devastation of her soul.

The things a woman often thinks she wants appear innocent enough, but they can destroy her. If our earthly desires are fulfilled, there can certainly be a sweeping exhilaration, but it will pass like the morning dew and leave us dried out and wasted away emotionally. It is only in the Lord that our hope will bring lasting happiness. Our hope in anything else is truly no hope at all. If we hope in wealth like Julianna, or security, a husband, children, a position, acceptance, friends, possessions, health; or if we put our anticipation toward where we live, what we do, the people we know; or if we desire a certain appearance, or reputation, or ministry, or recognition: it will never ultimately bring us the joy that hoping in the Lord alone can bring.

Envision a woman who can't help but smile because she knows something those around her don't know. That is us as Christians. We can always have a little smile because we know what awaits us as believers. As Christians we have the opportunity to have access to the very throne of the all-powerful God and to present our requests directly to Him in prayer.

We can hope with confidence in the Lord because we believe a glorious future is in store for us. One day we'll be transformed from corruption to glory. We can be hopeful because the Bible promises we will escape from eternal punishment in the lake of fire. Instead of judgment, we'll live eternally in the very presence of God where there will be no more tears or sorrow, but rather everlasting joy.

We can rejoice in our hope because we are being sanctified from sin and being made more holy. We've received forgiveness from God and

He's declared us righteous, just as if we had never sinned. We can rejoice in our hope because we are free from sin, and are not held captive by sin as slaves. We have fellowship with God and access into His presence, and an advocate with the Father, Jesus Christ the righteous. We've been freed from condemnation and given the gift of the Holy Spirit to dwell in us.

When we hope in the only true God, knowing there is no plan or purpose that can succeed against Him, we can be glad in our hope. Notice how Psalm 146:5 describes the person who knows he can find help in God: "Happy is he whose help is the God of Jacob, whose hope is in the LORD his God" (RSV). Our happiness comes from the knowledge of who God is, and that He is for us, if we are for Him.

And finally, we must rejoice in hope because the Bible directs us to. Romans 12:12 is a vital commandment to our health as Christians. It tells us to "rejoice in hope, be patient in tribulation, be constant in prayer". We rejoice in our hope because that is what pleases God for us to do, and He is so worthy of us doing what pleases Him.

CONTENTMENT IN WHAT GOD ALLOWS BRINGS JOY

Let me share a story with you about a time when I was not content. During the first few years of our marriage, my husband and I lived in a fourplex style apartment with a shared washer and dryer. Our unit was on a public street, which I had to walk down while carrying my laundry basket to get to the laundry room. At times I felt very embarrassed.

I remember telling people how much I disliked not having my own laundry room. My frustration with my laundry situation was really a frustration with where God had seen good for me to live. Instead of rejoicing that God had provided me a place to even do laundry, I murmured because it wasn't good enough! Instead of choosing to be thankful, I allowed myself to be bothered by something that was shamefully unimportant.

I remember a particular day when it was raining outside. My oldest son was a few months old and some of his clothes had to be washed. I strapped him in a baby carrier, picked up the laundry basket, and walked through the rain and down the street. As I was walking, I felt anything but thankful. I looked down at my son's face, expecting to see him ready to cry, and instead he was wearing a huge smile. While I was feeling sorry for myself, he was enjoying the raindrops and the fresh air. At that moment, I realized what a huge difference perspective makes.

When we grumble and complain against the Lord, instead of trusting Him with our current situations, we will be miserable. You may be asking, "How can a person be content when things are hard?" The first step is to consider where we place our focus. What thoughts do you think most often? Thoughts that are worrisome, filled with complaints or doubt, frustrated with people or situations, or that in any way are not being taken captive to the obedience of Christ will make it almost impossible for you to be content in the place God has you.

I may be thinking about how good and faithful God has been to me, and then only moments later become frustrated by something my husband or kids have done, and completely forget God is still faithful, even when the milk is spilled and I have more things to do than what feels possible. So the first step is having the right thoughts.

What thoughts should we have? If we are going to be content in all things, we must understand the wisdom, perfection, and sovereignty of God. We cannot allow ourselves to be deceived, thinking that what we want is greater or better than God's will for us. If I'm frustrated because one of my kids spilled the milk, for instance, my frustration reveals I don't believe in God's perfect goodness; that He allowed the milk to spill *for my good* (and probably my sanctification) because He is working "all things together for good, for those who are called according to his purpose" (Romans 8:28).

When we fight against God when things are difficult, foolishly absorb ourselves in our own desires, and mistrust God's goodness, our joy will be robbed and misery's entrance will be swift.

Isaiah 55:8-9 says, "For my thoughts are not your thoughts, neither are your ways my ways, declares the LORD. For as the heavens are higher than the earth, so are my ways higher than your ways and my thoughts than your thoughts." I believe really grasping what this verse says is crucial to the health of our emotions. The word *higher* used twice in verse 9 is the Hebrew word *gabahh* (gaw-bah'), and it means to be high, exalted, lofty. Dear beloved reader, ponder what this means. God's thoughts and ways are exalted over your thoughts and ways as the heavens are higher and more exalted above the earth.

One of our nearest stars, Sirius, a very bright star in the southern winter sky, belonging to the constellation Canis Major, is approximately fifty-four trillion miles from the earth. This is one of our closest stars, and it is fifty-four trillion miles away! The galaxy that we live in is about 587 quadrillion miles (5.9×10^{17}) in diameter.[1] And the known universe consists of about 200 to 300 billion galaxies![2] In other words, the heavens that God has created are *big*!

And this is the comparison of our thoughts to God's thoughts. If we can't even comprehend the size and length of the material heavens, how much more impossible do you think it is for us to comprehend and understand the ways of God? God's will is much better than our will because His thoughts and ways are much greater than what we can even understand or imagine. So when something happens in our life that makes us want to cry out *why*, we must believe that God allowed it in His wisdom which is greater than the heavens.

God inhabits eternity, and we dwell in a minutely small area of the universe, in a very small fragment of time with very limited understanding and a very small knowledge of only some things. God is the everlasting God, inhabiting one end of eternity to the other. He has infinite knowledge and understanding of all things. He knows what is happening in every place, at every time, throughout all time, even at this very time. Because God's knowledge is infinite, His ways are best.

This means God *knows* your financial problems, your marital despair, the arguments with your kids, the frustration with your living situation—God knows, and He allows these sandpaper patches in our lives so our faith might increase in smoothness. God uses our trials to polish us until we come forth as gold (Job 23:10).

I've found in my own life that when I resist trusting God with my sandpaper circumstances, they grow into jagged spikes and the trials only become more painful. Trusting God doesn't mean the trials go away, but that I believe God is good and concerned with me, though the trial is painful. And as God's precious children, we have a promise about painful trials. God chastens and disciplines those whom He loves so that we might partake of His holiness (Hebrews 10:5-10). The trials are for our benefit, to test and refine our faith, and to bring us forth as gold (1 Peter 1:6-7, Job 23:10).

I know from experience that being flexible and receiving what comes in life with thanksgiving is much easier than being anxious and frustrated. I've learned this through the many times I've first gotten frustrated when I should've been giving thanks. It satisfied my flesh to be irritated, but the end of irritability isn't joy. So let me clarify: when I say it's easier, I mean it's ultimately better when we respond to circumstances in a Spirit-filled way. It's often challenging to be flexible and thankful in the immediate situation, but reaping the harvest when you've sown seeds of thankfulness is much more enjoyable than reaping after having sown frustration.

There is great wisdom in obeying the commandment given to us in 1 Thessalonians 5:18, which says that we are to "give thanks in all circumstances; for this is the will of God in Christ Jesus for you." We don't know all that God is doing. We don't even know 1% of all God is doing. So when something happens that may otherwise make you want to scream, instead trust that God is working all things together for good for you if you love Him. Then you will be able to say with David, "I delight to do thy will, O my God: yea, thy law [is] within my heart" (Psalm 40:8 KJV). And if the will of God is for us to give thanks in everything, let us delight and rejoice in giving thanks.

When your heart feels anxious, or is not content to rejoice in what God is allowing, remember the exhortation in Romans 14:7-8 which says, "For none of us lives to himself, and none of us dies to himself. If we live, we live to the Lord, and if we die, we die to the Lord. So then, whether we live or whether we die, we are the Lord's." Since we are the purchased possession of Christ, we belong to Him. Belonging to Him disallows any justification of our resistance to what He desires for us.

We have been bought by God with a price, at the greatest cost ever known, the precious blood of His only begotten Son, Jesus the Christ.

> "Knowing that you were ransomed from the futile ways inherited from your forefathers, not with perishable things such as silver or gold, but with the precious blood of Christ, like that of a lamb without blemish or spot. He was foreknown before the foundation of the world but was made manifest in the last times for your sake, who through him are believers in God, who raised him from the dead and gave him glory, so that your faith and hope are in God" (1 Peter 1:18-21).

We don't own ourselves. As possessions of God it's our calling to submit to whatever He requires of us. As children of God, He has ordained both our salvation and the sacrifice of His beloved Son for our salvation. We are precious to God, and the evidence is the great price He paid so we would be His. He didn't call us to Himself so we'd spend our life in misery. It's true that a godly Christian will experience persecution (2 Timothy 3:12), but emotionally it's God's desire and commandment for us to rejoice and be content in Him. And even persecution is cause for rejoicing! Matthew 5:11-12 says, "Blessed are you when others revile you and persecute you and utter all kinds of evil against you falsely on my account. Rejoice and be glad, for your reward is great in heaven, for so they persecuted the prophets who were before you."

Glorifying God should be reason enough for contentment, so if being persecuted is what glorifies God, then it's possible to be content even in persecution. Contentment doesn't come by having everything we think we want, but by allowing ourselves to be satisfied with what God has chosen to give us. For this to happen, we must trust God. When our happiness is based on temporal things, it's fleeting: it comes and goes as what we have or don't have comes and goes. When our happiness is rooted in God, it's steadfast, regardless of what we have or don't have.

Being content begins with a thankful heart. It can be possible to desire change in your circumstances and still be content, but the desire for change should not make you unthankful, unbelieving, or cause you to decrease in the amount of love you show others, especially those closest to you.

By comparing our thoughts and actions with the scriptural standard, we can best discern whether we are pure in our desire for change. An impure desire for change is discontentment. An impure desire is ruled by fleshly and not spiritual cravings, evidenced by the way a woman reacts when change does not occur. If you are not content in your marriage, your lack of marriage, your job, your home, your position, your appearance, your location, or your life, you are sinning against God. One way to tell if you're being discontent is to scrutinize the way you talk or think about the situation. If you're mentioning to people how frustrated you are with whatever's bothering you, it's probably evidence of discontentment.

Have you taken time to give thanks for things that bother you, knowing God has allowed your life to be the way it is for a good purpose? Let your heart be like a bathtub that is continually filled with the waters of thanksgiving until your entire being is flooded. Be so filled with thanks that you flood thankfulness into every part of your life!

One lesson God has taught me over and over again is that I am always responsible for my sin, even if I am "provoked" to sin by someone else. In the garden of Eden, Eve provoked her husband to sin by offering him some of the forbidden fruit. But when Adam did eat the fruit, God held him completely responsible. A woman's bitterness and discontentment are never justified, even when her circumstances are miserable.

When Paul the apostle said he had learned to be content whether he was abounding or abased (Philippians 4:11-12), he really *understood abasement*. In Paul's second letter to the Corinthians, Paul described the afflictions he was facing, afflictions he was content with because he understood God's character in them:

> "Five times I received at the hands of the Jews the forty lashes less one. Three times I was beaten with rods. Once I was stoned. Three times I was shipwrecked; a night and a day I was adrift at sea; on frequent journeys, in danger from rivers, danger from robbers, danger from my own people, danger from Gentiles, danger in the city, danger in the wilderness, danger at sea, danger from false brothers; in toil and hardship, through many a sleepless night, in hunger and thirst, often without food, in cold and exposure. And, apart from other things, there is the daily pressure on me of my anxiety for all the churches" (2 Corinthians 11:24-28).

While it's easy to feel upset when things aren't going our way, especially when they're entirely outside our control, God still requires our complete trust in Him. He is jealous for your attention and your affection. While others may do things that frustrate you, God still wants you to be satisfied in Him. The more you feel frustrated, hurt, betrayed, used, disappointed, or forgotten by the people around you, the more opportunity you have to learn how patient, loving, kind, truthful, and attentive your God is.

Instead of complaining and murmuring in your heart about your circumstances, use the opportunities you have in your trials as appointments God has ordained for you to spend in prayer adoring Him. God will do what it takes to get your attention and your affection. Exodus 34:14 says, "For you shall worship no other god, for the LORD, whose name is Jealous, is a jealous God." God is more jealous over your affection and time than you are for the affection, time, praise, or respect of others.

Even if hurt has caused you to become cold, unloving, or even mean-spirited, God never becomes cold, unloving or mean-spirited toward His children. He still reaches out to us even after we have rejected Him countless times. Instead of focusing on what you want and need, focus on what you already have with a thankful heart. Despite what your relationship is with those around you, you have a God who longs for you. If you will draw near to God, He will draw near to you. He will be found by those who seek Him, and He alone is able to truly satisfy you.

No woman will ever be completely satisfied by her human relationships or situations, so it makes sense that a woman who seeks all her happiness in human relationships will have unfulfilled needs. God has not created us to be satisfied by others, but to be satisfied by Him. While God may sometimes use others to minister love to us, know that in God alone is complete fulfillment.

Part of learning to be satisfied by God is being humble. Without humility, you won't have any deep understanding of God's goodness, or the personal intimacy with Him that brings the greatest joy. God gives grace to the humble (1 Peter 5:5). When a woman joyfully submits herself to what God is allowing, she is demonstrating humility. She then takes upon herself the great opportunity of being able to anticipate grace from God. "God opposes the proud, but gives grace to the humble" (James 4:6).

And what else can we do in addition to being content and humble? We can pray! "The prayer of a righteous person has great power as it is working" (James 5:16). There is no such promise about discontentment! Make it a habit in your life that every time you desire to nag or comment or complain in your heart, that instead you pray effectually and fervently.

Then be patient and wait on the Lord. It's hard to wait if we don't believe God is a willing and able God. If we believe in God's power, and trust He will fulfill His plans for us, waiting becomes easier. The more we believe on God, the happier we'll be. Our source of joy shouldn't be things going well, but our source of joy should be the Lord.

And although God sometimes does reward contentment in Him with circumstantial joy, He doesn't have to. Someone who is satisfied in the Lord will, I believe, find that circumstantial joy comes easier. Small things can be tremendously satisfying to the heart that has already been satisfied by God. Picture the difference between two people, one who is satisfied by Christ, and another who seeks other means to be filled, while her cup remains empty:

>Two cups sat still on a shelf by the wall.
>As I glanced that way one sparkled, quite tall.
>It was much different from the next one, nearby.
>But because it was full it captured my eye.
>
>The other sat lonely, empty no less,
>longing and waiting, but unfilled, distressed.
>The first cup was sated, satisfied to its brim,
>the water had filled it, it sat no more dim.
>
>Dust had no place there, neither complaints nor doubt.
>Counterfeit fillers were cast quickly out.
>A small drop of water brought a happy reaction
>to the cup that abounded with much satisfaction.
>
>To the second, there was so much space left to fill.
>Every drop that went in showed what wasn't there still.
>No human pleasure made that cup overflow—
>disgruntled, upset, such a long way to go.
>
>If satisfaction were found at the true water source,
>that cup would be filled and cleansed with sweet force.
>But refusing true water and seeking mud sprinkles,
>the second's still thirsting and filled with dirt wrinkles.
>
>As I looked at the two, the contrast was great.
>Make me the first cup and my soul, satiate.
>Easily delighted seeking Your face;
>Make me content to rest in God's grace.

There is too much danger involved if you are not content where God has you. With all my heart, I exhort you, be content and rejoice! Don't desire to be in a place God hasn't put you.

My husband has a favorite saying, which he says often: "I only want what God wants for me. If God doesn't want it for me, then I don't want it." Since God is infinitely wise, why should we want something other than God's will? Instead of being disgruntled, rejoice at God's plan, even if it means hardship. Remember that God is working everything together for good for those who love Him. Whether it means being rich, poor, healthy, sick, famous, despised, welcomed, or cast out, rejoice because God knows what He's doing.

Let the Lord be your comfort and companion. If you're not satisfied in the Lord there's a great danger in looking for reassurance and satisfaction in unlawful sources, or letting loneliness, frustration, or worry usurp the worship of God in your heart, by focusing on what you don't have instead of worshipping *Him* whom you do have. Keep yourself pure! Delight to do God's will and let His law be within your heart.

~10~

Spiritual Labor

Addressing one another in psalms and hymns and spiritual songs, singing and making melody to the Lord with all your heart, giving thanks always and for everything to God the Father in the name of our Lord Jesus Christ.

Ephesians 5:19-20

Labor has a reward. When we labor to obey God more, we can't help but be blessed. Even when it's difficult to obey God—to trust Him when we can't see what's happening with our lives—it's still worth it. When we labor to fear God more, have wisdom, or wait on God, we will benefit richly in our lives and see our gladness increase.

FEARING THE LORD BRINGS JOY

I've never enjoyed horror movies. The idea of purposely scaring myself with spiders or convicts or zombies (or whatever it is horror movies use to scare people) has always been on my "no thank you" list. Because I personally don't find any enjoyment in being scared, why would I want to pursue fearing God more?

Fear and joy seem to be quite contradictory, don't they? Being terrified doesn't leave much room for happiness. Experiences that provoke fear usually don't leave pleasant memories. So why then would it be desirable to fear God? Wouldn't it just be better to love God and leave fear out of it?

But Scripture tells us that a person who fears God will be happy. "Happy is the man that feareth alway" (Proverbs 28:14 ASV). If this is the case, we must conclude that godly fear is different than earthly fear. While one is directed at earthly circumstances, the other is a fear founded in the knowledge of who God is. To have a proper view of what it means to fear God, let's first review who God is and what He's done for us.

God is always present and He is always aware of all that you do. He cares for you and He implores you to cast all your cares upon Him. He loved you when you were still His enemy and separated from Him. He called you before you ever even considered Him. He delights in you even though you are made of dust. He dances over you with singing even though you have nothing of yourself to give Him. He has freely given you all things that pertain to life and godliness. He has rescued you from the grasp of sin and death, and delivered you from His judgment so you could be His child. He loves you with an everlasting love. He has freely given you everything you need. And what do you have that you haven't received from Him?

God has been so overwhelmingly generous, good, kind, and loving toward us: so much kinder than we've ever deserved, and we deserve nothing but hell for all our sin and rebellion against Him. Even after He has so many times shown Himself strong on our behalf, yet again and again we waver in believing, and falter in obeying. "If we say we have no sin, we deceive ourselves, and the truth is not in us" (1 John 1:8). He has not rewarded us as our iniquities deserve, but He has poured out His loving kindness upon us.

We, in His goodness, have been chosen to be the objects of His mercy. Therefore, we are able to rejoice in all the goodness He has shown us. Yet, in His love, God has never closed His eyes to sin. Our sin had to be removed with the gruesome sacrifice of God's only begotten Son. Jesus had to die on a cross, and God had to forsake Him so that He (Jesus) might have our iniquities crucified with Him.

God has shown us immeasurable kindness, but to those who have not received the remission of their sins, the thought of God should be the most fearful and frightening of all their thoughts. The Bible says in Psalm 76:7, "But you, you are to be feared! Who can stand before you when once your anger is roused?" God hates sin and finds no delight in unrighteousness. Ponder what happens when God is roused to anger. "But the LORD is the true God; he is the living God and the everlasting King. At his wrath the earth quakes, and the nations cannot endure his indignation" (Jeremiah 10:10).

When God is angry, there is no one who can stand in His sight. As believers we have confidence that through the blood of Jesus we have escaped His wrath. "Since, therefore, we have now been justified by his blood, much more shall we be saved by him from the wrath of God" (Romans 5:9). But to the unbeliever there is no confidence of being saved from God's indignation. Where there is no justification through Christ's blood, there is no chance of escaping wrath.

We come boldly to God's throne of grace by faith, but God still requires our reverence. We must understand who He is so we respect and fear Him properly. If we do not fear God, we do not truly know God. Those who are the Lord's fear Him greatly. He is "a God greatly to be feared in the council of the holy ones, and awesome above all who are around him" (Psalm 89:7). God is holy and must be feared. The fear of the Lord is a necessary part of our obedience to Him. If we do not fear God, we are not wise. The fear of the Lord is the beginning of wisdom (Proverbs 9:10).

It seems almost impossible to define in words what the true fear of God is. God gives the believer a proper fear of Him, and that fear is a welcomed and pleasant fear. The fear of God causes us to run from evil and run toward Him. Fearing God gives us confidence that He is right in all He does and that obeying Him will be our strength.

When we fear God we are glorifying Him. The fear of God would include an awe of His coming judgments and wrath, but the fear of God makes a Christian cling all the more tightly to Him. God is great in power. He is worthy to be feared, and therefore we fear Him. But we fear Him with a confidence that He is our protector. Psalm 61:3 says, "For you have been my refuge, a strong tower against the enemy." For the righteous, we have God as our refuge.

Another reason we fear God is we know the wrath of God has been reserved for His enemies. The wicked have no refuge, and God will one day take wrathful vengeance on them. "The LORD is a jealous and avenging God; the LORD is avenging and wrathful; the LORD takes vengeance on his adversaries and keeps wrath for his enemies" (Nahum 1:2). The wicked who do not fear God are the ones who need to fear Him the most.

In fearing God we escape His wrath, and God blesses those who fear Him with many blessings. Psalm 115:13 says, "He will bless those who fear the LORD, both the small and the great." If we fear the LORD, He will deliver us out of the hands of our enemies (2 Kings 17:39). Those who fear God will be granted the amazing opportunity to be His friends. "The friendship of the LORD is for those who fear him, and he makes known to them his covenant" (Psalm 25:14).

Another blessing of fearing God is that "the angel of the LORD encamps around those who fear him, and delivers them" (Psalm 34:7). If you fear the Lord you will not lack anything you *need*. Psalms 34:9 says, "Oh, fear the LORD, you his saints, for those who fear him have no lack!"

This is an astounding list of benefits: We are blessed by God, made His friend, given understanding about His covenant, delivered from our enemies, given the angel of the Lord to deliver and protect us—and all this without lacking anything we need. Amazingly, the list goes on! God gives wisdom to those who fear Him. "The fear of the LORD is the beginning of wisdom, and the knowledge of the Holy One is insight" (Proverbs 9:10).

God uses the fear of Him to increase length of life. Proverbs 10:27 says, "The fear of the LORD prolongs life." The fear of the Lord coupled with humility can also bring riches, honor, and life (Proverbs 22:4). The fear of everything but God seems to come so easy for us, but if we can instead fear God alone, such a blessing awaits us.

Often God does mighty things for us so we will fear Him. God performed His wonders for the children of Israel so all the earth would know that God's hand is mighty, and that they might fear Him.

> For the LORD your God dried up the waters of the Jordan for you until you passed over, as the LORD your God did to the Red Sea, which he dried up for us until we passed over, so that all the peoples of the earth may know that the hand of the LORD is mighty, *that you may fear the LORD your God forever.*
> (Joshua 4:23-24, italics added)

God has surely shown His power in your life, whether you recognize it or not. And He has done it so you might fear Him. Fearing God is a prerequisite to true joy.

Fearing God preserves us from evil. Proverbs 16:6 says, "By steadfast love and faithfulness iniquity is atoned for, and by the fear of the LORD one turns away from evil." Sin and rebellion will produce misery, but righteousness is the source of life and joy. The woman who walks uprightly will have joy in her life as she is preserved from the misery sin brings. "Though a sinner does evil a hundred times and prolongs his life, yet I know that it will be well with those who fear God, because they fear before him" (Ecclesiastes 8:12). God will let it be better for those who fear Him, as those who fear the Lord hold a great advantage over those who don't.

A woman who fears God continually can be assured of His goodness in her life through every circumstance and trial, so fear the Lord and rejoice in the blessings God promises await those who fear Him.

WISDOM BRINGS JOY

Wisdom is an interesting thing. Wisdom can bring both vexation and happiness, sort of like human relationships. Solomon talks about this in Ecclesiastes 1:18, saying, "For in much wisdom is much vexation, and he who increases knowledge increases sorrow." The word *vexation* in this verse is translated from the Hebrew word *ka'ac,* and it means anger, provocation, grief, frustration.

Why do you think that having wisdom could be frustrating? I know I have been vexed when I see people around me suffering because of their sin, though they refused to forsake their sin. One example would be a woman who dates an unbeliever, suffers in the relationship, breaks it off, and then begins dating another unbeliever again.

I met a woman a few years ago right after she had been terribly beaten by her boyfriend. I tried to counsel her to break up with her boyfriend and walk with God, but she wouldn't receive what I was saying. She said she'd met her boyfriend right after he'd come out of jail for abusing his ex-wife. Part of me wanted to scream when I heard this. She was knowingly dating a man who was abusive, and to top it off, she was working full time to support him while he stayed at home. Now this woman was not a believer, but even common sense warns that a relationship like this would cause her to be miserable.

Looking in at her life, I could see all sorts of things destroying her. But she was completely blinded to her plight. If I was ignorant about why she was suffering, and if I couldn't see her reluctance to change, I guess I could have "blissfully" been her friend. But my understanding of what she needed to do, and her unwillingness to do anything about it after I'd told her, was vexing. It caused me grief that she refused to repent. So because of sin, wisdom can bring sorrow. It can also bring great joy.

Proverbs 3:13 says, "Happy is the man who finds wisdom, and the man who gains understanding" (NKJV). And five verses later Proverbs 3:18 says regarding wisdom, "She is a tree of life to those who take hold of her, and happy are all who retain her." The woman who walks with understanding and whose heart is set to please God will have joy.

There are two types of wisdom, in a sense. The first is heavenly wisdom; it descends from God and is based in truth. Worldly wisdom, the type James speaks of as "earthly, unspiritual, demonic" (James 3:15) is a false wisdom; this wisdom thinks it's right when it's not, because it leads away from God instead of towards Him. "The wisdom of this world is folly with God" (1 Corinthians 3:19). It is the "the mere working of natural reason, without any supernatural light."[7] This fleshly wisdom is not the type of wisdom I'm promoting for our joy.

From this point on, when I talk of wisdom, I am only referring to the wisdom from above (James 3:17). A woman with godly wisdom doesn't consider herself to know everything, but her wisdom makes her very aware of how much more she has to learn.

Wisdom is a wellspring of life, and from it springs joy and many other blessings in abundance, and it is very deep. God rewards those who have wisdom, and God is the giver of wisdom. According to Proverbs 4:7, wisdom is the principal thing. Therefore, with wisdom being the primary thing, let's get wisdom!

Besides giving joy, wisdom is advantageous because it preserves life. The advantage of wisdom over money is explained in Ecclesiastes 7:12: "For the protection of wisdom is like the protection of money, and the advantage of knowledge is that wisdom preserves the life of him who has it." Money and all treasure can never give life, but wisdom is more excellent because it has life to give. A wise woman understands how to conduct herself so her life is preserved in this life and in the time to come.

She is like a person with clear vision, able to discern where she is going. Solomon, the wisest person who ever lived besides Jesus, made many observations about wisdom. He contrasted a wise person with a foolish person, saying, "The wise person has his eyes in his head, but the fool walks in darkness" (Ecclesiastes 2:14).

He also compared wisdom to a sharpened ax. If you are cutting down a tree with a dull ax head, more strength is needed; if your ax is very sharp, your work is easier. In the same way, wisdom is profitable to direct. He explains this saying in Ecclesiastes 10:10, saying, "If the iron is blunt, and one does not sharpen the edge, he must use more strength, but wisdom helps one to succeed."

The source of all wisdom and understanding is always the Lord, for wisdom has been with Him from the beginning, and He gives wisdom. In Christ "are hidden all the treasures of wisdom and knowledge" (Colossians 2:3). James 3:17 says, "But the wisdom from above is first pure, then peaceable, gentle, open to reason, full of mercy and good fruits, impartial and sincere." Spiritual wisdom abounds with life to those who have it, in gentleness and without harshness. The increase of heavenly wisdom, knowledge, and understanding is a powerful spring and fountain of joy!

A person who lacks wisdom will find joy in foolish things, and the wicked will find their delight in sin. This is because "folly is a joy to him who lacks sense" (Proverbs 15:21). The pleasure that comes from folly is that which brings death, and the consequences to those who sin with joy and without repentance will be severe. "She who is self-indulgent is dead even while she lives" (1 Timothy 5:6). While a wise woman is like a tidy, secure house with the lights on, a self-indulgent, foolish woman is like a broken house that's been long abandoned, being already ready for demolition even while it stands.

But wisdom makes the first house secure, giving life and joy to those who possess it. If we desire to be filled with joy, we must search and obtain wisdom as the primary thing. Our source of wisdom is God, and the fear of the Lord is the beginning of wisdom. Humble yourself, fear God, and ask for wisdom, and He will give it generously (James 1:5). The Holy Spirit gives us spiritual understanding, which is eternally profitable. If we'll diligently give ourselves to seek wisdom early, to hear her instruction and to follow it, we will find a multitude of blessings as God has promised.

DESIRE FULFILLED AFTER WAITING BRINGS JOY

One difference between rejoicing because of circumstances and rejoicing at all times is rejoicing always takes faith! Rejoicing by faith means being glad even before seeing the fulfillment of our desire, accomplished by placing our hope upon the living, faithful God.

There will likely be times we wait on the Lord without even knowing what God's will is for us concerning our desire, but we must trust that what He has for us is best. It's easy as humans to always want something we don't yet have and spend our time trying to get it. What are you longing to see happen in your life? Are you waiting on the Lord with frustration or with peace?

Often we wait anxiously because we have a hard time really trusting in God. Yet when we believe that His thoughts toward us are for good and not for evil, to give us a future and a hope, we can wait patiently and confidently upon our God.

In the Old Testament, Abram's wife Sarai desperately wanted a child. The story starts in Genesis 12:1 when God tells Abram to depart out of the land of Haran and go to a place that God would show him. Let's carefully notice the age of Abram and his wife, Sarai, throughout this story, so we can appreciate more of its significance. Genesis 12:4 says, "So Abram went, as the LORD had told him, and Lot went with him. Abram was seventy-five years old when he departed from Haran." Sarai was ten years younger than her husband, making her sixty-five at this time.

Now Abram and Sarai had never been able to conceive children, but at this time God promises Abram that he will have a child and will make of him a great nation. Genesis 12:7 says, "Then the LORD appeared to Abram and said, 'To your offspring I will give this land.' So he built there an altar to the LORD, who had appeared to him." Again, God made Abram the promise that he would have a child in Genesis 13:15-16, saying, "For all the land which you see I give to you and your descendants forever. And I will make your descendants as the dust of the earth; so that if a man could number the dust of the earth, then your descendants also could be numbered" (NKJV).

As time goes by, Abram begins to doubt God's promises, and he reminds God of his wife's barrenness, saying, "Behold, you have given me no offspring, and a member of my household will be my heir" (Genesis 15:3). God again reassures Abram of His promise to him, saying, "This man shall not be your heir; your very own son shall be your heir" (Genesis 15:4). We might hope there would be no doubt in Abram and Sarai's mind that they *were* going to have a son, but doubting is easier than faith.

Ten years pass, and still Sarai has not conceived a child. But instead of patiently waiting on God, she attempts to make what she wants to happen come to pass by doing things herself. She asks her husband to sleep with her maid Hagar, to conceive a son through her. Abram consents to her wishes and Hagar has a son named Ishmael. Genesis 16:16 says Abram was eighty-six when Ishmael was born, making Sarai seventy-six years old.

Yet this son Ishmael was not the child of God's promise, but he was the child of Sarai's work in her flesh. Because of Sarai's haste to get what she wanted (yes, ten years is haste if it's not God's timing), the result was great sorrow and distress. Sarai had to reap bitter consequences for not waiting on God. The son born to Hagar was a wild man, and he and his descendants persecuted Sarai's son and descendants for many years, even to this day (Genesis 16:12).

Ishmael wasn't the child of God's promise, but he was a picture of bondage, because he was the child of the bondwoman Hagar. God did not honor Sarai's own rush to get what she wanted done by letting the child of her impatience fulfill His promise. But He did allow the child to partake in the allegory of our freedom apart from the law. Ishmael represents that which is born after the flesh, and is in bondage.

When we act in haste apart from waiting on God, our actions will be of our flesh, and may result in great sorrow and distress for us. But if we allow God to do His work, and believe on Him, the result will be our joy and His glory. Even though Sarai faltered in believing God, God did not falter in fulfilling His promise to her. "If we are faithless, he remains faithful—for he cannot deny himself" (2 Timothy 2:13).

When Abram was ninety-nine years old, God again appeared to him and reaffirmed His promise. God changed Abram's name to Abraham, which means "father of a multitude," because Abraham would be the father of many nations (Genesis 17:5). God also changed Sarai's name at that time also to Sarah (Genesis 17:15), and said to Abraham, "I will bless her, and moreover, I will give you a son by her. I will bless her, and she shall become nations; kings of peoples shall come from her" (Genesis 17:16). Sarah was now eighty-nine years old, but God told Abraham, "I will establish my covenant with Isaac, whom Sarah shall bear to you at this time next year" (Genesis 17:21).

Fifteen years after Sarah acted in foolishness and haste, and twenty-five years after God first gave her the promise, Sarah did have a son from her own body. Genesis 21:1-3 says, "The LORD visited Sarah as he had said, and the LORD did to Sarah as he had promised. And Sarah conceived and bore Abraham a son in his old age at the time of which God had spoken to him. Abraham called the name of his son who was born to him, whom Sarah bore him, Isaac." Abraham was one hundred years old when Isaac was born, which made Sarah ninety years old when she had her child (Genesis 21:5).

Sarah had to wait twenty-five years for the Lord to fulfill His promise to her, but the Lord did do what He had promised. Isaiah 25:9 says, "It will be said on that day, 'Behold, this is our God; we have waited for him, that he might save us. This is the LORD; we have waited for him; let us be glad and rejoice in his salvation.'" I can only imagine Sarah's joy when she did finally give birth to the child she'd waited so long to bear.

After God told Sarah she would have a baby, she still had to wait a long time. Often, we think we are patiently waiting on God, but our prayers are something like this: "I don't at all mind waiting for the baby You promised me Lord, as long as in nine months I'm holding him in my arms!"

Sometimes a very long wait is involved for the things God has promised us, but when what we've been waiting for comes to pass, joy is the natural result. Proverbs 13:12 says, "Hope deferred makes the heart sick, but a desire fulfilled is a tree of life." When God fulfills our desire, we cannot help but rejoice! God is faithful, and we must hope in Him, believing joyfully that He will bring what He has promised to pass.

~11~

Restoration

See that no one repays anyone evil for evil, but always seek to do good to one another and to everyone. Rejoice always, pray without ceasing, give thanks in all circumstances; for this is the will of God in Christ Jesus for you.
1 Thessalonians 5:15-18

Restoration is the act of restoring, refreshing, and bringing back something or someone to its original state. Whether we've lack holiness or felt condemned, it's God's desire to restore our soul. Growing up in church, I became very familiar with the words David penned in the 23rd psalm: "The LORD is my shepherd; I shall not want. He makes me lie down in green pastures. He leads me beside still waters. He restores my soul" (Psalm 23:1-3).

Possibly your mind is familiar with the words, "He restores my soul," but does your heart know it? Has your soul been restored by God after you've heard some devastating words or said the regrettable words yourself? Have you been restored after doing something you said you'd never do? Have you been released from the guilt of a past failure or do you still need your soul restored?

I don't want to imagine where I'd be if God hadn't restored my soul after each and every one of my many failures. Our God is faithful. He is able to restore our hearts when pain has shredded them; to restore our joy when sin has eaten it; to restore our faith when trials are drowning it. He is the restorer of our souls.

THE JOY OF RESTORED HOLINESS

Holiness is being set apart to God from sin. Things that are holy are things that belong to God, and God is holy. And God has called us to be holy even as He is holy. First Thessalonians 4:7 says, "For God has not called us for impurity, but in holiness." Though the righteousness of Christ has been imputed to us, we can lack holiness in our thoughts and behaviors.

When we're not abiding in God's holiness we'll become very worn out. Sin brings weariness and sorrow. Sinful thoughts and habits that separate us from God must be removed, because they can effectively leave us feeling discouraged and strip our lives of holiness and joy. God has set us apart to holiness. The things that are not pleasing to God in your life must be severed if you're going to draw near to God in sincerity.

Because I've already dealt with the subject of sin robbing us of joy in chapter 4, I want us to see how to have our joy restored after it's been sapped by sin. What does a woman do once she is reaping the consequences of discouragement and dismay? She may feel raw, and because of the penalties of sin she may be defenseless and exposed. It's at these times she most needs a shelter. God in His holiness can be the only shelter that will provide true protection from the storm. Isaiah 25:4 says, "For you have been a stronghold to the poor, a stronghold to the needy in his distress, a shelter from the storm and a shade from the heat." God is the only shelter that will truly comfort and revive us.

There is no stability apart from God, for He alone does not change. So when we come to Him for our protection, we can find a stable, secure place to hide. He desires to be both our refuge and our hiding place. He wants us to find our refuge in Him alone until destruction passes by, even if we are the cause of the destruction. He promises that if you draw near to Him, He will draw near to you (James 4:8). Don't be afraid that if you come near to God, He will reject you.

If you are failing in hope because you've lacked holiness, come to the rock who is higher than you. Find refuge in the God who is a strength to the needy in distress. Then, as God is your comfort and refuge, your heart can be revived. He will lead you so that you don't err in the same paths you've erred in before, if you'll trust Him and follow Him with your whole heart. He will be your guide, leading you to streams of waters and into cool pastures. He will gently guide you if you will follow Him completely.

After Clara allowed some "innocent" exposure to worldly standards into her heart, she needed to make God her refuge. She was a woman who earnestly desired God, but a momentary lack of resistance was able to penetrate her contentment deeply. One day, while strolling around the supermarket, she took a turn down the magazine aisle. A headline from one of the women's magazines drew her attention, and she discretely stashed the magazine in her shopping cart. It was uncharacteristic of her to buy that sort of magazine, but she was lured by a headline.

It seemed harmless enough to her; she would only read her article and then throw the magazine in the trash. After all, she reasoned, it would be easy for her to discern what would be bad for her to expose herself to, anyway. When she got home, she read her article, but then curiously flipped through a few more pages. She read a couple more articles, and began to notice how beautiful all the models were. Without thinking, she stared at their bodies and thought of her own. She threw the magazine away, but the images stuck in her head.

Soon she got a little sad every time she looked in a mirror. She started worrying about the size of her thighs, something she'd once happily forgotten. How she looked began to take priority in her life, and she began to use money she couldn't afford to spend for maintaining her appearance, which made her more depressed. What seemed like an innocent "peek" at a worldly standard had robbed her of contentment.

Rachel also found herself in a place of uneasiness after allowing a little "harmless" flirting in her life. It was only weeks after celebrating her fifteen-year anniversary with her husband that she met George, the new manager of her division at her office. She didn't think much about him at first. But after a while, she noticed he seemed to be wherever she'd go. He began to compliment her, not too much, but enough that she wanted more. He told her she had dazzling eyes and that he loved her intelligence, something her husband didn't appreciate much. It wasn't long before Rachel looked forward to seeing him.

Her heart pounded a little heavier when she knew George would be around, and soon she was working overtime just to see him. *I can't help what I feel*, she insisted to her heart, and she began to allow her imagination to wander. One moment she would reprimand herself for even thinking about George, and the next moment she would imagine a conversation in which he confessed his love to her. It became a vicious cycle that devastated her. She could no longer seek the Lord like she had before, and the harmless box of flirting she'd opened longingly exposed a giant ticking time bomb, waiting to destroy her soul. She knew she had to take drastic measures before it was too late.

Pouring out her heart and all her emotions to the Lord, Rachel purposed that she would do all she could to avoid George. She knew if she did not make the Lord her refuge, this mighty storm of destruction would come with devastating vengeance, leaving nothing left standing in its path. She began praying earnestly that God would remove all her unlawful feelings. As she prayed, she began to feel that maybe God was calling her to transfer to a lower position in a different office.

This was something she did not want to do, but the more she prayed that God would just take her feelings for George away, the more she knew she needed to physically be away from him. Sadly but determinedly she put in her paperwork for a transfer and was moved within a few weeks.

She no longer saw George and her feelings for him subsided. She was then freed from the crushing emotions of illicit love, and she praised God for His deliverance in helping her escape what could have destroyed her life.

Both Clara and Rachel found themselves in bondage, robbed of freedom and joy, without having committed any obvious sin, at first. I used both these two women's stories because they began so innocently; neither one began with a direct rebellion against God's commands. In both of these cases there was a very fine line between what was right and what was wrong.

Often it's hard to see what actions will lead to unholiness in our lives, and unless we are being fully obedient to the Spirit of God, sometimes a weight can begin to grow in our lives before we even realize it's there. It's possible for us to miss the lack of holiness invading our hearts because the circumstances are not severe. Clara's story is not extreme, and most woman can relate to insecurity with their appearance. I'm sure many woman have also dealt with wanting to receive the affections of another man, as evidenced by the high numbers of adultery, fornication, and divorce in our society.

We have the option to run to the Lord as our shelter, or compound sin upon sin by not making the living God our place of safety. If a woman chooses, for whatever reason, not to run straight to the holy arms of God when she becomes aware of her bondage, then she is doing the thing that pleases herself more than the thing that pleases God, and she can expect to feel desolate and worn. The ways of the Lord are not burdensome. His yoke is easy and His burden is light. If you are in a rough place because you have sown iniquity, remember that God is gentle. He is kind even to the unthankful and the evil. He does not reward us in this life as our iniquities deserve, but He is kind (Psalm 103:10; Ezra 9:13).

He "is the Savior of all people, especially of those who believe" (1 Timothy 4:10). God saves and prolongs the life even of those who do not love Him. God shows kindness even to His enemies, so how much more assurance do we, as His friends, have of His kindness and acceptance of us. And God has called us to holiness because of His kindness. He understands so much better than us the destruction of sin. His commandments for us not to sin express His love for us and His protection of us. When we obey His commandments, and walk in holiness, there is safety and joy. God commands us to be holy because He is kind, because He cherishes us, and because He is love.

The Bible comforts us with a promise of the gentleness of our Messiah, Jesus. Upon realizing the error of our sin, often we can feel like a piece of grass that has just endured a painful crushing by an unaware hiker. Our once sturdy stalk has been injured, and we feel it would not be surprising if we presently broke in half. The sweetness of our Savior is that, when we are crushed, He will not destroy us. Instead He will restore. Isaiah 42:3 says, "A bruised reed he will not break, and a faintly burning wick he will not quench."

We may be bruised and faintly burning, but God will not lay upon us more suffering than we can bear, to quench us completely. Jesus knows our frame, sympathizes with our weaknesses, and when we feel like our fire is about to be extinguished, God can fan us into a flame if we'll allow Him.

God delights in you, and desires to see you delight yourself in Him. Because we cannot foretell all the consequences of our sin, God makes it easy and commands us to be holy. Separate yourself to God and come out from all uncleanness and iniquity. If you will keep yourself pure, and be holy as He is holy, you will find a wellspring of joy springing up in your life that is beyond what words can describe.

Instead of allowing yourself to feel downcast because of circumstances, choose to rejoice at all times because your heart so loves God that you dare not sin against Him. My prayer for you is that, as you realize what a shelter and safety God is to the brokenhearted, you will cling to the Lord above all things, so that any weariness in your heart will be traded for joy and delight in the God who redeemed your very life!

THE JOY OF NO CONDEMNATION

"There is therefore now no condemnation for those who are in Christ Jesus" (Romans 8:1). In the presence of the Lord is fullness of joy, so in the Lord's presence there can be no condemnation, because condemnation brings sadness and lethargic depression.

Condemnation can come from many places and has several meanings. The first is the condemnation that comes from God: This condemnation is God's judgment on those who reject Him, and the punishment or condemnation is death and hell. People under this condemnation cannot experience true joy, because they are alienated from the life of God. A true believer will not be under God's condemnation, because he has passed from death to life.

Romans 5:16-17 says,

> And the free gift is not like the result of that one man's sin. For the judgment following one trespass brought condemnation, but the free gift following many trespasses brought justification. If, because of one man's trespass, death reigned through that one man, much more will those who receive the abundance of grace and the free gift of righteousness reign in life through the one man Jesus Christ.

Adam's sin in the garden of Eden brought death to all men and judgment to condemnation. A person escapes this judgment leading to condemnation by receiving the gift of righteousness, which happens at salvation. If you are under the first type of condemnation, the condemnation of God to judgment, the escape is salvation.

The next type is the condemnation of the law. The law condemns a man because it plainly states what God has commanded people to do and not to do, and when we see ourselves in the light of God's law, we see the abundance of our own sin. Second Corinthians 3:9 refers to the law that came from Moses as the "ministry of condemnation." The law condemns us as we become aware of the commandments we've broken. If you experience the condemnation of the law, study the ministry of righteousness (2 Corinthians 3:9) and believe that the righteousness of Christ has been imputed to you. If you continue in this condemnation because of sin, then forsake your sin.

Condemnation can also be self-imposed through guilt. It comes to those whose faith falters, as they begin to look at their own sinfulness apart from the righteousness of God imputed to them. Condemnation occurs in believers' hearts when they begin to think they have something good of themselves, and they forget all their goodness comes from God alone. Then, when their own goodness is not as good as they would like it to be, condemnation results. The cure is faith.

When we have this condemnation, it is our way of trying to serve the punishment for our sin. We use feeling badly to "earn" God's favor again, and this is the same as trying to attain righteousness by our own works. God's anger toward sin is not appeased by our self-condemnation and our feeling badly. God does not punish us for our sins, but His wrath has already been appeased when He poured it out on Christ.

Jesus appeased the coming wrath of God toward us who believe on Him. First Thessalonians 1:10 says Jesus "delivers us from the wrath to come." There is no longer any wrath from God toward us for our sin, and we are only wasting time and sinning when we linger in guilt. Instead of self-pitying condemnation, we need to be filled with godly sorrow that leads to repentance, and trust that Jesus endured the punishment for our sins in our place.

If we in any way trust our own righteousness to make us holy, we will have no righteousness at all. "Now to the one who works, his wages are not counted as a gift but as his due" (Romans 4:4). Therefore, to walk blamelessly before God, free from all condemnation, we must receive His righteousness and believe that all our holiness is truly His holiness. Apart from Him, we can do nothing (John 15:5).

There is no righteousness or goodness we can offer to God from our own human storehouses. We can only receive by faith His righteousness imputed to us. If you allow yourself to feel bad as a way to earn God's favor, confess this to God and forsake any hope you place in yourself. This third type of condemnation does not please God and will stifle you from abounding in gladness. If you are under condemnation because of guilt, you must take your eyes off yourself and put your complete faith and trust in God.

Lastly, the fourth type of condemnation results from what you allow. People can bring themselves into condemnation by doing something they are not convinced they should do. If you allow yourself to partake of something that is not contrary to Scripture, but may be considered a grey area as to whether it should be allowed, only do it if you are sure you will do it with faith. "For whatever does not proceed from faith is sin" (Romans 14:23). But when you partake of what you know God has approved of with faith, you will be happy. Why? Because that is what God has declared in Romans 14:22, saying, "Hast thou faith? have [it] to thyself before God. Happy [is] he that condemneth not himself in that thing which he alloweth" (KJV).

If you're troubled in your heart, then do not sin against God by participating in something that makes you feel condemned. If you do have faith, let it be between yourself and God so that other believers do not stumble. But if you feel guilty about doing something, or you fear it may be sinful, or what you're doing is not being done in love or for God's glory, it cannot be done in faith and must be avoided. Rejoice in the measure of faith God has given you, and be happy in what you allow and are convinced is God's will for you. And if you're condemned by what you allow, prayerfully seek the Lord about what you may need to give up. Have a heart that will do anything necessary to glorify God.

THE JOY OF TRUSTING GOD THROUGH THE RESTORATION

Have you ever had financial problems? If yes, you probably know how hard it sometimes is to trust God in those times. Let's say a woman has no money to pay bills because her husband has spent the money on a new laptop computer that's nonrefundable. What can she do? She can worry or she can rest. If she chooses to worry, it's likely she'll be disrespectful toward her husband and inwardly turmoiled.

She can *choose* to rest, but how? By believing God has her situation under control and not thinking about what's already been done. Trusting God in hard situations means believing He is good, even if her car were to be repossessed and the creditors kept calling. It means being willing to rejoice even while her world may seem to be falling apart.

When an issue is pressing hard in your soul, rest confidently in God who is always faithful. Often it is easy, and temporarily satisfying, to act hastily upon our emotions without regard to wisdom, but he that handles the matter wisely will be rewarded for it. This means that although we may want to do what *we* want to do when *we* want to do it, if we do what God wants us to do when He wants us to do it, things will turn out better. And what is the reward of trusting God in every trial? God's Word confidently says that the person who trusts in God will be happy: "Whoso trusteth in the LORD, happy [is] he" (Proverbs 16:20 KJV).

One way to tell if you're trusting the Lord or trusting in yourself is by taking your "gladness" temperature. Use the amount of joy you have as a thermometer to gauge your level of trust in God. If you find that you're unhappy, recognize you need to increase your trust in God: Whether it's trusting that His love for you is beyond comprehension, His will for you is perfect, His thoughts about you are unceasing, or just remembering that even right now God is thinking about you and He hasn't forgotten you.

As simple as this sounds, its elementary truth is foundational. If you come to God and trust Him, believing He will take care of all your cares and not even a bird falls to the ground and dies apart from Him, it will be much easier to rejoice. A stressed out, worried heart has no place for joy.

But a restful heart that trusts the only One who is truly trustworthy can easily rejoice.

The more a woman knows her God with experiential understanding, the easier trusting God in difficult situations becomes. David knew that trusting God and rejoicing were both mutually necessary; one could not survive without the other. "The LORD is my strength and my shield; in him my heart trusts, and I am helped; my heart exults, and with my song I give thanks to him" (Psalm 28:7). We must trust in Him even before we see His answer.

If we wait to see His deliverance before we trust in Him, it's not trust at all, but the attitude of the multitude in Capernaum who said to Jesus, "Then what sign do you do, that we may see and believe you? What work do you perform?" (John 6:30). They thought if they saw a sign, they would believe. But Jesus answered them, saying, "But I said to you that you have seen me and yet do not believe" (John 6:36). They saw Jesus in the flesh and they still did not believe Him; so even if Jesus had done a miracle, He knew their thoughts, and that they would not believe. There were many people who *saw* Jesus do miracles, and yet still were faithless.

Therefore God requires that we believe in Him apart from seeing Him, and that we place our trust in Him because we come to Him by faith and not by sight. "Though you have not seen him, you love him. Though you do not now see him, *you believe in him and rejoice* with joy that is inexpressible and filled with glory" (1 Peter 1:8, italics added).

Our faith in God is directly related to our joy, and the more we trust Him the happier we'll be. Think about how you'd react if you received an unexpected bonus at work, or won a large sum of money that was completely unanticipated. No one would have to tell you to be joyful, because that emotion would come naturally. Yet we have received salvation and eternal life. More than even that, we have received every spiritual gift there is! "Blessed be the God and Father of our Lord Jesus Christ, who has blessed us in Christ with every spiritual blessing in the heavenly places" (Ephesians 1:3).

The gifts we've received so far outshine worldly benefits that it would make sense for us to be blinded to all temporal gains. Our joy in the Lord is to be far superior to the delight we'd experience from receiving unexpected money. Even though we would most likely rejoice at the money, the value of knowing Christ is so much more, because His value is so much greater than any amount of money! Do you believe the greatness of the gifts you've received? We should be more ecstatic about God's heavenly gifts than earthly treasure. The measure of our joy reveals the measure of our faith. Truly receiving by faith the gifts God has given will bring abundant joy.

Using your "joy thermometer" to gauge your trust in God (Proverbs 16:20), is there room to trust the Lord more in your life? Identify the areas in your life that most easily discourage you. Determine to trust God's power and control over those concerns. Romans 15:13 says, "May the God of hope fill you with all joy and peace in believing, so that by the power of the Holy Spirit you may abound in hope."

It's possible to abound in hope even when the things in this life seem to be going terribly wrong. Shortly after her eighth birthday, Janice's house caught fire and consumed almost everything her family owned. It happened suddenly, after a spontaneous combustion in her garage. Soon the house was engulfed in flames as she stood helplessly outside. It shook Janice to her core and it was many years before she did not daily fear another fire.

As an adult, Janice still occasionally feared a fire, although much less often. She had learned through her experience to trust with more confidence in the perfection of God's ways; and God had also graciously blessed her since then. Her husband, Kurt, was a godly man who adored her, and they had just moved into a brand new beautiful home with picturesque mountains behind them.

It was on a Tuesday morning, while Kurt was at work, that Janice was alone at home reading her Bible when thoughts of fire again began troubling her. She thought to herself, *How would I react if my new house caught fire?* She lifted her eyes up to heaven, and prayed, "Lord, You are God. I know You are love and that You work all things together for good to those who love you. Blessed be the name of the Lord. I will trust You no matter what You give, or what You take away."

She glanced back down at her Bible and read, "God is our refuge and strength, a very present help in trouble. Therefore we will not fear though the earth gives way, though the mountains be moved into the heart of the sea" (Psalm 46:1-2). With tears of reassured trust streaming down her face, she glanced out her window and looked at the hills.

Suddenly she realized with great shock that the fire she had been presently musing on was real, and it was quickly approaching her house. Within seconds she also heard the sound of fire-truck sirens outside her house. In a split second she was both overcome with fear and then calmed as she reminded herself that "though he slay me, yet will I trust in him" (Job 13:15 KJV). With only her Bible, journal, and a few photo albums, she was safely outside.

A fireman led her down the street to wait. In what seemed like a dream, she stood with the very neighbors she had recently shared Christ with and watched as the fire leaped onto her fence and climbed around to the side of her house. She couldn't see the side of her house that was burning, except for the flames shooting up from the roof.

Janice's thoughts drifted back to the faithfulness of God in actually preparing her for this moment right before it happened. She was startled out of her thoughts when her neighbor, Marty, asked her why she was smiling. She hadn't been aware she was smiling, but she didn't want to lose this opportunity to share with this lady who previously had shown no interest in Jesus. With so many thoughts cramped into her head, she wasn't quite sure what to say, so she just began talking.

"Why are you not falling apart when your brand new home is?" questioned Marty.

It wasn't that Janice was happy her home was on fire; if anything, she was devastated. But she rejoiced because she knew God had both allowed the fire (because He could have stopped it) and that He would work all things together for good for her. She knew that despite the fire, God was still faithful. She told Marty these thoughts as best she could utter.

When she was done talking, Marty noticed a fireman walking toward them. He reported that the fire was extinguished completely. It had come from the hillside behind her house, burning her fence, living room, and entryway, but had not spread to any of the neighbors' homes.

Janice called her husband at work and told him all that had happened. Their lives became very busy for a few weeks, but they were able to quickly find an apartment to live in until their house could be repaired. During that time, about a week after the fire, Janice received an unexpected call at work from Marty. She asked Marty to come over to her apartment as soon as she got home from work.

Marty did come straight over. And before even sitting down, Marty began to tell Janice that although her own house had not been affected by the fire, she'd been so moved by Janice's trust in God she'd barely slept all week. She wanted Janice to explain all about her God so she might know Him herself, and that day Marty became a new creation in Christ!

After Marty left, Janice fell down to the floor with rejoicing because she knew God had softened Marty's heart to salvation in a way nothing else could have. Marty began meeting weekly with Janice to be discipled, and Marty also started going to church faithfully.

A few weeks later, only an hour after Janice's husband Kurt had left for work, she saw him walking back up the walkway to their apartment.

"What's going on?" she cheerfully questioned, as she opened the door to let him in.

"I just got laid off," he told her, matter-of-factly and without hesitation.

At first, Janice was overwhelmed with worry. It had been hard for them to make both the mortgage and the rent payment, and she knew there was no way they would make it now with him out of work. She was more in disbelief than anything.

Within a few days, she noticed herself becoming more irritable. She began to doubt that all things were working together for good. She had trusted God through the fire, but this seemed like it might be more than she could handle. Money grew scarcer until they had literally none left, and both the mortgage and rent payments were due again.

Although Janice seemed to be praying constantly that God would provide, she realized she wasn't doing it with complete trust. If she'd been trusting completely in God, she'd have been able to rejoice and wouldn't have been irritable. She did desperately want to rejoice, but this time the joy was not coming like it had before. She realized she needed to choose to rejoice in God's faithfulness, and be glad in His greatness now more than ever, especially because she couldn't understand it.

She turned some worship music on in her living room and set her heart to sing the praises of God. She was so involved in freely praising God that she jumped with fright when the doorbell rang. When she opened the door, the mailman had a letter she had to sign for. After he left, she opened the envelope mechanically and almost screamed when she realized it was the check from their insurance company for the fire damage. Relief accompanied calculations. She went through the math and realized they'd received quite a bit more money than the estimates she'd received for work on their home. She then understood how God had used the fire to sustain them while her husband would be out of work.

It took more than two months for her husband to find a new job—an amount of time that would have been impossible for them to endure without the insurance money. And the new job her husband got was also much better than his previous one; he was getting paid a higher salary to do something he enjoyed more. He also met two Christian men in his office that he prayed with at lunchtime.

It was another month before their house was repaired and they were able to move back in. As Janice sat in her living room once more, Bible and journal in hand, she stared out the window and prayed: "Oh Lord, thank You that you allowed me to see some very good reasons why You allowed the trials that You did. My help doesn't come from the hills, but from the Lord, the maker of heaven and earth. You alone are my help. You are my shield, my fortress, and my deliverer. I will praise Your holy name, because You are forever worthy to be praised."

Looking down at her Bible once more, she stopped knowingly, with much awe, at Job 42:12, "And the LORD blessed the latter days of Job more than his beginning." For the times she had chosen to put her trust in God and rejoice by faith, despite the difficulty of her circumstances, she was now flooded with all the emotions of joy and gladness. She had learned experientially: "Behold, we consider those blessed who remained steadfast. You have heard of the steadfastness of Job, and you have seen the purpose of the Lord, how the Lord is compassionate and merciful" (James 5:11).

~12~

Beyond Our Control

For his anger is but for a moment, and his favor is for a lifetime. Weeping may tarry for the night, but joy comes with the morning.

Psalm 30:5

*I*n this chapter I discuss three ways to obtain joy that don't quite fit in the other chapters. All three of these ways to obtain joy are often beyond our control.

First we'll look at how joy can come when those we influence bear fruit in Christ. But though we can faithfully reflect Christ and explain the gospel to people around us, there is no guarantee we'll always see the fruit of it in this life.

The second part of this chapter deals with trials and sufferings. Though we may live a commendable life, hardships and heartbreaks may still crash unavoidably upon us.

The final subject of this chapter is when God just freely heaps joy right into our laps as a gift. In these cases we just rejoice because God makes us rejoice, and it's nothing we had any part in. In Christ, sometimes we win the spiritual lottery without even buying our own ticket. God gives us the ticket and then declares us the winner. And because of His goodness, we get to enjoy the jackpot.

SEEING THE RIGHTEOUS LIVES OF THOSE WE'VE BROUGHT TO THE LORD BRINGS JOY

This subtitle was tricky. What I really wanted to call this section was "Seeing the righteous lives of those we've brought to the Lord brings joy; seeing faithfulness to Christ in the lives of people we've ministered to brings joy; planting a seed and later seeing the harvest of righteousness in a person brings joy; preaching the gospel to someone and hearing about their salvation brings joy." But alas, fifty-four words is a bit much for a subtitle in a chapter.

Still, they are all true. Faithfully ministering the gospel of Christ, and seeing the fruit of righteousness in people who've received the Word gladly, that is cause for great joy. Paul expressed his joy over the Philippian believers, saying in his letter to them, "Therefore, my brothers, whom I love and long for, my joy and crown, stand firm thus in the Lord, my beloved" (Philippians 4:1).

Paul himself had first brought the gospel of Jesus to Philippi, after receiving a vision of a man asking him to come to Macedonia and help them. Philippi was a leading city of the district of Macedonia and a Roman colony. There Lydia was converted.

After Paul cast a demon out of a slave girl who told fortunes, her masters were so upset they dragged Paul and Silas before the magistrates and had them beaten and thrown into prison. At midnight, while Paul and Silas were praying and singing hymns to God, an earthquake opened all the prison doors. The jailer and all his household believed in Jesus that night, and in the morning Paul and Silas were asked to leave the city. After saying goodbye to Lydia and the brothers, they departed (Acts 16:9-40).

The letter to the Philippians was written eleven years later, to the church Paul had established there. He rejoiced as he wrote this letter to them, because they'd remained steadfast in the Lord those eleven years.

First, in Philippians 1:3-5 Paul says, "I thank my God in all my remembrance of you, always in every prayer of mine for you all making my prayer with joy, because of your partnership in the gospel from the first day until now." Paul was so thankful for this church, even from the first day they partnered in the gospel to now when he writes this letter. He rejoiced every time he thought of them or prayed for them. He remembered them in prayer with a thankful and happy heart!

Second, Paul rejoiced over the Philippians because of his labor and sacrifice for their faith. He describes this in Philippians 2:16-18 saying he holds "fast to the word of life, so that in the day of Christ I may be proud that I did not run in vain or labor in vain. Even if I am to be poured out as a drink offering upon the sacrificial offering of your faith, I am glad and rejoice with you all. Likewise you also should be glad and rejoice with me." Paul rejoiced over the Philippians because they remained steadfast in the Lord, because he had fellowship with them in the gospel, and because they were his dear brethren.

In writing to the Thessalonians, Paul again states they are cause for his joy. First Thessalonians 2:19-20 says, "For what is our hope or joy or crown of boasting before our Lord Jesus at his coming? Is it not you? For you are our glory and joy." The believers at both Philippi and Thessalonica were Paul's glory and joy. "For now we live, if you are standing fast in the Lord. For what thanksgiving can we return to God for you, for all the joy that we feel for your sake before our God" (1 Thessalonians 3:8-9). As we witness righteousness abound in the lives of those we have led to Christ or have ministered to in their growth, what a cause for joy!

This joy can be both a present rejoicing and a cause of eternal gladness. "On the day of our Lord Jesus you will boast of us as we will boast of you" (2 Corinthians 1:14). Our glorying over one another's righteousness should be mutual, as both a cause for rejoicing in our temporal bodies and also a cause for rejoicing on the day of the Lord Jesus.

That steadfast, wise apostle John said he found his greatest joy in the faith of his children. "I have no greater joy than to hear that my children are walking in the truth" (3 John 1:4). Both good parents and good ministers will rejoice at the genuineness of their children doing what is right.

Barnabas also had joy over the saints. Acts 11:23 says, "When he came and saw the grace of God, he was glad, and he exhorted them all to remain faithful to the Lord with steadfast purpose." Are you gladdened by the faithfulness of others to the Lord? To what degree do you rejoice at the steadfastness of other saints? David, speaking concerning the joy that others would have at his own faithfulness, said, "Those who fear you shall see me and rejoice, because I have hoped in your word" (Psalm 119:74).

It's interesting to me that, sometimes, the righteousness of others becomes a conduit to jealously or competition instead of compelling us to rejoice. There are two paths we can take when approached with the steadfastness of another believer. There is a sinful path, and it can be mined with many types of iniquity. Instead of rejoicing at the exaltation of another's righteousness, we can feel bitterness, jealousy, feelings of being left out, and much more. This path will not only bring destruction to our own souls, but can potentially be very defiling for others also.

The other path is rejoicing with the sister who has stood fast in the Lord, because she is a member of the same body as we are. Even if she is honored and praised above us, we rejoice, because her joy is also our joy. When one member is honored, all the members should be glad, because their honor is our honor (1 Corinthians 12:26). This is the biblical and right path, and it's the example set by other saints before us.

The more we love one another, the more we'll naturally rejoice with each other. Our days are numbered, the return of Christ is imminent, and time is short. This life is a vapor, so let's do what we must do to please God with all our being, loving one another fervently.

TRIALS AND SUFFERINGS CAN BRING JOY

Now some people might ask, "Aren't joy and suffering contrary to each other?" And for an unbeliever I would say the answer is an emphatic yes. The world cannot understand joy in intense suffering. They have no reason to be glad when everything is going wrong. But let's read what Peter describes as the experience of Christians in their suffering. First Peter 1:6-8 says,

> In this you rejoice, though now for a little while, if necessary, you have been grieved by various trials, so that the tested genuineness of your faith—more precious than gold that perishes though it is tested by fire—may be found to result in praise and glory and honor at the revelation of Jesus Christ. Though you have not seen him, you love him. Though you do not now see him, you believe in him and rejoice with joy that is inexpressible and filled with glory.

Notice what's causing the heaviness: various trials. The word *trials* in verse 6 is also translated into the word *temptations*. It's not that the believers in this particular passage are simply experiencing trials. There are many trials we experience that could be considered "easy" because we're strengthened to bear them. There have been times when I've gone through what could be considered hard, and yet my soul was not in "heaviness" at the trial.

When my oldest son was about eight months old, my husband got laid off from his job. He was able to get a new job quite easily, but it was two hours away, and we were forced to move. At that time we were in escrow to purchase a new home that was still being built. Plus, most all of my family and close friends lived nearby, so moving meant giving up our new house, my family, our friends, and our church we loved.

This situation could have been very difficult for me, but I wasn't in heaviness over the trial. I knew God was the One who saw fit for us to move, so I left sadly, but not despairingly. Instead of being discouraged, I was able to enjoy the change and even rejoice. Sometimes easy things can be quite hard on us emotionally and hard things can be easy. What it's very possible Peter is speaking of in this verse is more than just trials, but when the trials seem unbearable.

Have you ever felt utterly overwhelmed by your circumstances or difficulties? In times of suffering intensely, there can be such an immense weight of heaviness, it may feel almost intolerable. When all your energy is gone and grief consumes you, this is the trial of your faith. Faith is tried because we must believe in God's wisdom, control, and love over our lives when things are hardest to understand. The trial is in holding on and believing when the suffering distresses both our temporal circumstances and our eternal faith.

Consider Jesus, who was "anointed with the oil of gladness above his fellows" (Hebrews 1:9 KJV). This same Jesus who knew greater joy than any living person also experienced sorrow to the point of death: Matthew 26:36-39 says,

> Then Jesus went with them to a place called Gethsemane, and he said to his disciples, "Sit here, while I go over there and pray." And taking with him Peter and the two sons of Zebedee, he began to be sorrowful and troubled. Then he said to them, "My soul is very sorrowful, even to death; remain here, and watch with me." And going a little farther he fell on his face and prayed, saying, "My Father, if it be possible, let this cup pass from me; nevertheless, not as I will, but as you will."

If you've ever experienced deep pain and sorrow, be comforted that Jesus also experienced sorrow to the point of death. We are the body of Christ, and we are to be like the head in both His joy and in His sorrow.

When Job was in the midst of tremendous suffering—every one of his children had been killed, he'd lost all his possessions, his body was in agonizing pain and covered in boils, and his wife had told him to curse God and die—he refused to sin against God and said instead in Job 19:25-27, "For I know that my Redeemer lives, and at the last he will stand upon the earth. And after my skin has been thus destroyed, yet in my flesh I shall see God, whom I shall see for myself, and my eyes shall behold, and not another. My heart faints within me!"

When our faith is being tried by fire, it's all the more important that we believe in who Jesus is. Even in suffering we can still rejoice in the return of our Savior, and love Him even though we do not see Him. Though it may be easy to focus on the distressing circumstances, to feel angry because your husband doesn't walk with God, or because he's stumbling in the walk he does have, or because your child has rebelled and is spiraling downward, or because you're dealing with a situation at work or with your family that isn't being resolved, and these things haven't changed after many years of waiting, it's at these times you must actively increase your faith and do everything you can to believe all the more that God's Word is true. Encourage yourself in His Word, knowing you're going to receive the salvation of your soul!

The salvation of our souls is the end of our faith. One day we'll be walking by sight. One day we'll *see* our Savior's face! We must cling to this hope to sustain us. Paul said knowingly in Romans 8:18, "For I consider that the sufferings of this present time are not worth comparing with the glory that is to be revealed to us." Paul went through terrible sufferings, and endured beatings, imprisonment, starving, and worse, yet he knew the glory to be revealed to him could not even compare to the sufferings he endured.

One of the greatest of all Paul's sufferings can be found in Romans 9:2-3, where Paul said he had "great sorrow and unceasing anguish" because of the unsaved Israelites. I don't believe anything can potentially cause more pain than losing a loved one to eternal torment. Paul said he'd give up his own salvation if it meant his brothers, the Israelites, would be saved! (Romans 9:3).

So much of our hope in this life during trials is bound around the solid pillar of a future in the presence of God. The strength for Christians in suffering is the understanding that glory will soon be revealed in them.

Sometimes this can be bittersweet, if we dwell on those who reject Jesus as their Savior. So before I proceed to talk about the joy of heaven, I want to address the issue of eternal torment.

As in all things, we must find our answers in the Bible. Only verses after Paul shares the anguish he feels over his unbelieving brethren, he goes on to declare God's sovereignty as triumphant over all his human grief. It's very interesting to me that Paul moves from the subject of the glory to be revealed in us (in Romans 8) to the sorrow he has over the lost (at the beginning of Romans 9) to the reason *why* God has done it all the way He has (the rest of Romans 9).

In other places in the Bible, Paul acknowledges that people will go to hell because they are justly deserving of punishment (1 Corinthians 6:9-10). In this chapter, Paul expands on something that is often hard for our finite minds to comprehend, but something we will one day understand completely.

In verse 11 of Romans 9, Paul reports that people are chosen by God before they've ever done any good or evil so God's purpose of election might stand. The eternal misery of the lost is not something I take lightly, but let me tear out my tongue and cut off my fingers before I dare reply against God or try to tone down what God has declared in power, by explaining the meaning to be less than what God Himself has said it is. Paul, by the inspiration of God, words it this way:

> So then he has mercy on whomever he wills, and he hardens whomever he wills. You will say to me then, "Why does he still find fault? For who can resist his will?" But who are you, O man, to answer back to God? Will what is molded say to its molder, "Why have you made me like this?" Has the potter no right over the clay, to make out of the same lump one vessel for honored use and another for dishonorable use?
>
> (Romans 9:18-21)

Eternal punishment is possibly the "harshest" truth in the Bible, but we can't ignore truth because it's offensive. While there is extreme punishment and suffering reserved for some, there is extreme delight and joy for others. Some people would like to take this part of Scripture and hide it under a bushel. I would like to say that because this is the Lord's doing, let it be marvelous in our eyes! (Psalm 118:23). Eternity with God will be the most glorious thing we could ever receive!

For those who refuse to receive God's free gift of salvation because they will not forsake their sin, to them the pleasure of this life will be fleeting and the heavy weight of the suffering and eternal misery of hell will never end. The heaviness of the believer is but for an earthly season, but the heaviness of the unbelievers will come, and with greater force than they have ever known in this life, and it will never end. How much better to suffer in this life, knowing the sufferings of this present time are not even worthy to be compared with the glory which shall be revealed in us, than to walk in the amusement of sin now, but then to depart from God eternally into everlasting fire at the end of your fleeting time on earth?

Those who are apart from Christ and do not know God Paul describes as "having no hope and without God in the world" (Ephesians 2:12). The dark subject of hell must be often addressed, just as the night must often come, but once it has passed we can rejoice all the more when the light of day comes. The light dawns and we see more clearly the hope of our glorious future against the backdrop of night. We have hope that the world apart from God will never experience or understand. I believe I can summarize it this way: God is to be glorified when people go to hell as much as He is to be glorified when people go to heaven. And as I have talked about hell, I now want to glory with you in God's goodness in choosing some to go to heaven!

In the book of Revelation, John describes the holy city we'll one day dwell in, saying, "No longer will there be anything accursed, but the throne of God and of the Lamb will be in it, and his servants will worship him. They will see his face, and his name will be on their foreheads" (Revelation 22:3-4). One day we'll gaze upon the one we now love.

Therefore it's of great importance that while we wait for Him, our hearts rejoice, because even though we can't see Him, we know He's coming quickly. Second Corinthians 4:17-18 says, "For this slight momentary affliction is preparing for us an eternal weight of glory beyond all comparison, as we look not to the things that are seen but to the things that are unseen. For the things that are seen are transient, but the things that are unseen are eternal." For the Christian, we have an eternal hope, and our trials are but for a moment compared to eternity.

Even when we're immersed in suffering, we can rejoice. But how? How do we rejoice always in the midst of difficult trials and suffering? The answer is found in Peter's exhortation: "Though you have not seen him, you love him. Though you do not now see him, you believe in him and rejoice with joy that is inexpressible and filled with glory" (1 Peter 1:8).

We rejoice in our trials because we believe in God. First John 3:2-3 says, "Beloved, we are God's children now, and what we will be has not yet appeared; but we know that when he appears we shall be like him, because we shall see him as he is. And everyone who thus hopes in him purifies himself as he is pure."

What is the source of our great rejoicing? It's our belief in Him whom we have not seen! Faith is absolutely essential to joy. True, lasting joy has its foundation firmly rooted in faith.

Even when our hearts are burdened beyond measure with grief and the trials of this life, we must find our refuge in the Lord. The darker and dimmer times may seem, the more it's necessary we walk by faith and not by sight. If we only find our joy in temporal things, it will be easily depleted.

Remember the trial is "for a season" (1 Peter 1:6 KJV). It may be for a few hours, weeks, years, or even a few decades—but there is a greater and exceeding eternal weight of glory that awaits us, and the trial will end. All trials for the believer will end, and God is faithful. We will soon look upon His face and behold the One we love.

Even in the hardest of circumstances, God has given us His Word to cling to. Psalm 30:5 says, "For his anger is but for a moment, and his favor is for a lifetime. Weeping may tarry for the night, but joy comes with the morning." Psalm 126:5-6 says, "Those who sow in tears shall reap with shouts of joy! He who goes out weeping, bearing the seed for sowing, shall come home with shouts of joy, bringing his sheaves with him." The end result of our depending on and clinging to God in our trial will be joy. And when the trial passes, we'll come forth like refined gold, filled with rejoicing.

As we're in trials, or as we look ahead to the day when we'll experience great trials, we can be confident of two things. The first is—we can be confident God is keeping us. Peter says in 1 Peter 1:3-5,

> Blessed be the God and Father of our Lord Jesus Christ! According to his great mercy, he has caused us to be born again to a living hope through the resurrection of Jesus Christ from the dead, to an inheritance that is imperishable, undefiled, and unfading, kept in heaven for you, who by God's power are being guarded through faith for a salvation ready to be revealed in the last time.

God is not depending upon our righteousness to keep us, but He Himself is keeping us. You have great cause for rejoicing in your suffering, because "He who began a good work in you will bring it to completion at the day of Jesus Christ" (Philippians 1:6). God has obtained our eternal redemption for us and it is reserved by Him. In the darkness of heaviness we are not left alone to keep ourselves, but we are "kept by the power of God through faith unto salvation" (1 Peter 1:5 KJV).

The second reason for our confidence is knowing the trial is working in us. Deep sorrow can be used in preventing a Christian from becoming too proud. When we have all we need in this life, we can forget it was from God's hand alone. So He allows trouble sometimes, and then, in our trouble we cry out to God, and from our depths He hears us. Suffering is good for us. We learn in suffering how to have compassion. C. H.

Spurgeon said, "There are none so tender as those who have been skinned themselves. Those who have been in the chamber of affliction know how to comfort those who are there."[1]

James 1:2-3 says, "Count it all joy, my brothers, when you meet trials of various kinds, for you know that the testing of your faith produces steadfastness." In heaviness we must throw ourselves upon the truth of the Word of God. Through believing we rejoice. When we meditate upon all the goodness God has shown us, and we consider the time is soon that we will look upon Him whom we love, we can rejoice even in the heaviness of our souls.

We will not always walk by faith. Very shortly we will walk only by sight, and all our opportunity to believe in Him by faith will have passed. The day is coming soon when our own eyes shall behold our Lord Jesus. We'll see with our own eyes the scars by which He obtained our eternal salvation, bringing us into a relationship with Him. We will be bodily in the very presence of God who created the heavens and the earth!

Job understood this and said, "And after my skin has been thus destroyed, yet in my flesh I shall see God" (Job 19:26). Just think with me about the moment we'll first look with our eyes upon Jesus. How exciting it is to think about that moment! My heart beats faster when I remember I'll be with Him forever.

And we will be like Him and see Him as He is. This life will have been only a moment, and then we'll see Jesus, who was sinless and yet endured great suffering and the death of a cross to make us the righteousness of God in Him.

Remember, we are righteous through faith in Jesus. We have no condemnation, but rather we have an advocate with the Father, Jesus Christ the righteous. And our inheritance awaiting us is incorruptible and undefiled, reserved in heaven for us. And so we rejoice greatly because our hope is great, and the glory we'll have in eternity is beyond what even words can express. We say "Even so, come quickly Lord Jesus, come quickly" (Revelation 22:20).

GOD GIVES US JOY AS A GIFT

According to 1 Corinthians 4:7, there's nothing we have or possess we didn't first receive. So when we experience any joy at all, it's God's gift. We don't deserve to receive joy, but God puts joy in our heart freely because *He is good*! The gift of joy we receive from God is greater than the joy found in earthly or temporal gifts. David affirms this in praise to God, saying in Psalm 4:7, "You have put more joy in my heart than they have when their grain and wine abound." David proclaims it's God who has put joy in his heart. He compares his gladness to the happiness of others when their grain and wine increase.

The present day comparison would be that the joy God can put in our heart is better than the fleeting happiness of riches. Rejoice and enjoy the Lord more than if your riches were to multiply.

God gives us joy, and it is much, much better than earthly gain. In Psalm 30:11, David acknowledges his joy comes from the Lord, saying, "You have turned for me my mourning into dancing; you have loosed my sackcloth and clothed me with gladness." David is turned from sorrow and grief to joyful dancing, and his covering becomes gladness. He has been girded in joy from the Lord. Therefore in Psalm 30:12, David responds to the Lord in response for all that God has done for him, saying he would "sing your praise and not be silent. O LORD my God, I will give thanks to you forever!"

I can't help imaging that David's joy surfaced in a smile so large it consumed his face. Have you ever smiled like that, where you're smiling so big your skin can't take any more? Now have you smiled like that in response to the Lord?

A woman who refuses to take the time to recount God's goodness, and thank Him for it, might never enjoy a smile like that. Consciously making yourself aware of the specific things God has done for you is vital to giving thanks forever. As you purposely focus on why God is worthy of praise, praising Him will become compulsory. God is worthy of our eternal thanks and gratitude. He has blessed us with so many gifts, both spiritual and physical, and one of those gifts is joy. When you receive joy from the Lord, do not hesitate to give thanks unto Him who is worthy to be praised.

The joy we do have is from God, and He can put more gladness in our hearts than the wicked have when their riches increase. Though David came to the Lord empty, with mourning and sackcloth, God filled him with dancing and rejoicing. The joy of the believer is filled with hope. Our joy is bound up in God who will never change (Malachi 3:6), and He gives us joy freely because He is good, and that will never change.

~13~

Devoted Maintenance

Through him then let us continually offer up a sacrifice of praise to God, that is, the fruit of lips that acknowledge his name.

Hebrews 13:15

*H*aving concluded our study of *how* to obtain joy, let's now turn our focus to the specific times in life *when* the Bible specifically requires us to be glad.

JOY IS REQUIRED WHILE EATING AND DRINKING

Food brings pleasure, and that satisfaction we get from eating is a gift from God. He desires us to rejoice and enjoy the food He gives us. Ecclesiastes 9:7 says, "Go, eat your bread in joy, and drink your wine with a merry heart, for God has already approved what you do." When you eat and drink, do it with a thankful and rejoicing heart.

In Acts 14:17, Paul says the living God "did good by giving you rains from heaven and fruitful seasons, satisfying your hearts with food and gladness." God has given us food as His gift. And 1 Timothy 6:17 says to trust not "on the uncertainty of riches, but on God, who richly provides us with everything to enjoy." Don't despise food, and don't sinfully idolize it, but receive your food with thankfulness and gladness, and rejoice while enjoying it, thanking your Lord Jesus Christ and God the Father through Him.

BEING GLAD WHEN WE'RE WITH OUR HUSBANDS

Sometimes it's easiest to give into feelings of frustration and worse when we're around our spouse, but the Bible says mates are called to live joyfully together all their days. Ecclesiastes 9:9 says, "Live joyfully with the wife whom thou lovest all the days of the life of thy vanity" (KJV). God's design is for couples to find joy in marriage, but in some cases, or at certain times, rejoicing with your spouse is at the zenith of "impossible" commands.

When we're pleased with our husbands, then we're willing to show them love and rejoice in their presence. But when they do something that hurts us or frustrates us, I think sometimes we excuse our lack of love for them by their actions. Justifying our lack of joy, we think it's okay for our behavior to be affected by their behavior. We assume it's excusable if we sin as a result of their sin. It's not. No matter what our husbands do, our lack of continual joy is still sin.

It is a deceptive lie to think God excuses frustration and bitterness toward any other person because of that person's actions. If we're to love those who we don't know as ourselves, how much more should we love the one to whom we have been joined together as one?

During those times when it's hardest to be joyful in the presence of our husbands, we must resist the desire to yield to sin. In obedience to God we must continue to rejoice. This is where we must choose to rejoice no matter how we feel. Make a list of verses you can take refuge in and rejoice in, and meditate on them whenever you would be tempted to sin by grumbling against the Lord.

Never let the circumstances of this life cause you to cease rejoicing. Though our hearts will rejoice at things "worthy" of being rejoiced at, our joy should not diminish when those things are diminished. It's much better to speak to yourself in psalms, and hymns, and spiritual songs, singing and making melody in your heart to the Lord (Ephesians 5:19), than it is to nag your husband and be a contentious wife. The first will please God, and the other will cause God to resist you. (Because only by pride comes contention, and God resists the proud [Proverbs 13:10; James 4:6].) The first one will be effective in changing your husband (1 Peter 3:1-2), and the second will only harden his heart toward you.

Even if he does change by your nagging, it will come at the price of separating the unity in your marriage and possibly causing bitterness and a decrease in your husband's affection for you. So when you would want to nag or be grumpy to get your way, instead trust that God who knows all things also knows what will work best. Then let your husband see your own fear of God through your obedience to Him. This is what will be most effective in changing your husband.

Now let me add—from my own experience I know that it's *hard* to rejoice always, especially when my husband may not be doing what I want him to do. Though I feel like wanting to show him I'm upset by acting downcast, the Holy Spirit still reminds me to rejoice always. I've had to learn, sometimes on my face, that I need to rejoice always no matter what's happening to me or around me. I have had to learn that I can't ever let the actions of other people cause me to sin. I need to be holy before the Lord despite what any other person in all the world does. This is why I emphasize so often how necessary it is for us to keep our minds fixed on things above.

And regardless of how angry or upset I may want to get at a situation, I still have to be filled with love, joy, peace, patience, kindness, goodness, gentleness, faith, and self-control (Galatians 5:22). I've also learned from experience this can be almost impossible if I'm not set on glorifying the Lord Jesus Christ at any and every cost. Even when I fall short of this goal, I know it's God who will keep me and complete me. Precious sister, He'll also do the same in you. The Bible says that God, who has began a good work in you, will be faithful to complete it (Philippians 1:6).

Just as we need to rejoice in the presence of our husbands, we also need to rejoice when others are happy—which brings us to our next section.

REJOICING WHEN OTHERS ARE JOYFUL

Imagine you accomplished some great deed for your country. The President decided to honor you with a special medal. With your head held high, you hear the loud applause of a huge audience. The President leans near you and places the medal around your neck. With joy filling your heart, you believe nothing could ruin this grand moment.

Suddenly you begin to hear your mouth spewing out complaints about what's happening! Grumbling, it protests angrily against that lucky neck who *always* gets the medals. You're appalled, because your neck and your mouth are both members of the same body—yours! With frustration, you try to clamp your hand over your mouth to quiet it, but your hand shakes itself bitterly at the neck as well.

What's happening to me? you wonder frantically. *Don't my hands and mouth understand they're all part of one body?* When your eyes look up, you realize everyone in the audience is staring at you, speechless and stunned. Your mouth gapes open in horror from making such a fool of itself.

You desperately hope your body will cooperate, and this time it does. Every member sympathizes with the embarrassment you're feeling. Your whole body is ready to fall into a heap of sobs, shaken by your awful experience.

Have we imagined a situation that seems too absurd? Sadly not. Though our physical bodies are typically cooperative, the spiritual body of Christ can be another story. It's easy to become jealous or disgruntled when another person is honored. It's harder to rejoice at the blessings of others than our own blessings. In our selfishness, it's natural for us to want good things, or want at least as much as what others are getting—but when someone *else* gets the good things and we get nothing, it can be hard to feel genuine happiness. If we've been longing for a new car, and someone at church shows up with the car we've been wanting, sometimes it's hard to feel joyful.

But as Christians, we're all one body in Christ. "For just as the body is one and has many members, and all the members of the body, though many, are one body, so it is with Christ" (1 Corinthians 12:12). As such, it's the design of God for us to be glad even when others receive gifts and we don't.

Part of loving one another as you love yourself is rejoicing with others in their joy and excitement, just as you'd rejoice in your own joy and excitement. Romans 12:15 says, "Rejoice with those who rejoice, weep with those who weep."

God has designed us with feelings, especially as women, so we can share emotions with each other, bear one another's burdens, and so fulfill the law of Christ (Galatians 6:2). We need to genuinely care for each other. Paul wrote to the Corinthians, saying, "If one member suffers, all suffer together; if one member is honored, all rejoice together" (1 Corinthians 12:26).

My husband and I have a friend who has spent many of his years studying doctrine. Though he is very gifted in defending the Christian faith, for years doors only seemed to be shut toward him and his desire to teach the Bible. Then, after many years of waiting, he was given a chance to participate in a debate and preach the gospel. When the time came, he not only refuted every unbiblical argument seamlessly, but also shared the gospel with the audience clearly and boldly.

I was so happy for him: His long awaited desire to speak publicly had finally come to pass; and he had done so well. Afterward he was honored with praise, and although I am not fond of heaping praise on any person, I was glad for him to be honored.

The body of Christ is one body, and so when others are joyful, we are called to be joyful, too. And just as the whole body would mourn if the hands were injured, so we all mourn with one another. Sometimes rejoicing with those who rejoice can be harder than mourning with those who mourn, because often we're mourning with those who have it worse than us; but when we rejoice with others, it's often the case that they have something we don't.

When Jan's husband received a raise from his employer, Jan excitedly called her good friend Reba. As Jan was telling Reba her good news, Reba acted happy for Jan, but inwardly she was in turmoil. She found it hard to be sincerely glad for Jan, because she knew her own family needed a raise much more than Jan needed it. How could Reba really rejoice with Jan, when she herself was missing out on what seemed good? Reba's selfishness hindered her ability to share Jan's joy.

A selfish woman is happy when she gets what she wants, but she finds it hard to be happy when others get privileges and she doesn't. A woman who desires above all things to please God will rejoice with those who rejoice, without evaluating how fair the situation may seem. Circumstances shouldn't dictate how happy a woman is toward others who rejoice, but instead a woman should be governed by the biblical standard of Romans 12:15.

The ultimate reason Reba or any of us should rejoice is that Christ is the head of the body. We are the members, not the head, and so any honor that the body receives truly belongs to Him. Our calling is not to please ourselves, but to please God who chose us. Even when our feelings get hurt and people disappoint us, our happiness needs to be centered around pleasing God because He is the One we live for.

HAPPINESS WHILE SERVING GOD

Any position of service to the Lord should always be done with rejoicing. Psalm 100:2 says, "Serve the LORD with gladness! Come into his presence with singing!" Serving the Lord in itself can be a great source of joy, but we are to have joy while serving whether or not the joy comes from what we are actually doing. The more we understand what a high calling it is to serve the Lord, the easier joy comes. God is honored when we serve Him joyfully, and as we long to honor God, we can rejoice as we serve.

If we're serving for earthly admiration, and not joyfully in obedience to God, it will certainly ruin our focus at least, and can leave us depressed, miserable, and burnt out at the end. God can be served by so many things we might do, and God is honored when He sees us serving Him happily.

The Bible says man looks on the outward appearance (1 Samuel 16:7). With our propensity to look on what's outward and seen, the human inclination is to think God is most honored when we're most praised. Yet God does not look on the outward appearance. He looks on the heart, and the praise of man does not in any way commend us to God. Jesus said in Luke 16:15, "You are those who justify yourselves before men, but God knows your hearts. For what is exalted among men is an abomination in the sight of God."

The greatest honor does not and cannot come from man, because the honor of man is fleeting, restless, and prone to change. The weighty honor that comes from God is eternal and unchangeable. Honoring God is not contingent on being seen and honored by people, but God looks at the heart, to see if a woman is truly honoring Him with her motives and longings. If a woman is seeking the honor of people, she can't truly be honoring God (Galatians 1:10).

God will honor the person who serves Him. Serving God is higher and better than serving people. We don't need to serve Christ in honorable positions to be honored by God. The Bible doesn't say we are honored by our position, but because we are serving Jesus. Set your heart right, that in serving your desire would be to serve Christ, and God the Father will honor you.

If you are the person at your church who folds the bulletins, cleans the windows, sweeps after the service, or straightens the chairs, and nobody sees you—God will honor you for serving Him. Jesus said "If anyone serves me, the Father will honor him" (John 12:26). Some of our works will be wood, hay, and stubble. But some will be gold, silver, and precious stones, and we will be rewarded by God in eternity for those works. Let's not strive for the honor in this life that's only a fleeting vapor, but let's seek the honor of God that will be ours in eternity.

In Matthew 25, Jesus tells a parable about a man who gives his servants money to invest for him while he is gone. To the first servant he gives five talents of silver (a talent was a large amount of money), to the second he gives two, and to the last he gives one. The first two men were faithful servants, and traded their money until it was doubled. The last servant buried his money in the ground and did nothing with it. When the lord of the servants returned, he commended the first two, saying to each, "Well done, good and faithful servant. You have been faithful over a little; I will set you over much. Enter into the joy of your master" (Matthew 25:21). The wise servants received praise and honor; the foolish servant was severely punished.

Like the wise servants, if we are faithful to God, joy will be reserved for us as a reward of serving Him devotedly in the area He's appointed for us. Those who are obedient to what God has called them to do are fulfilling an honorable role. Whether you consider your area of ministry as small, or look upon another's area of ministry as small—since we can't see the big picture, don't despise what God is doing. Do not despise what you probably don't know. God's ways are so much higher and greater than our ways.

We are both to serve God faithfully in whatever he has called us to, and also honor those who serve. First Peter 2:17 says, "Honor everyone." This is necessary. First, we are to honor those whom the world is not accustomed to honoring as much as we are to honor the rich or famous person we may meet at some time in our lives. James 2:1-4 says,

> My brothers, show no partiality as you hold the faith in our Lord Jesus Christ, the Lord of glory. For if a man wearing

a gold ring and fine clothing comes into your assembly, and a poor man in shabby clothing also comes in, and if you pay attention to the one who wears the fine clothing and say, "You sit here in a good place," while you say to the poor man, "You stand over there," or, "Sit down at my feet," have you not then made distinctions among yourselves and become judges with evil thoughts?"

Partiality toward someone for his position in this life will make a woman a judge of evil thoughts. Let the believer of low degree be exalted!

Luke 1:52 says that God "has brought down the mighty from their thrones and exalted those of humble estate." James 1:9 says, "Let the lowly brother boast in his exaltation." If you serve the Lord with gladness of heart, and you do it willingly, even though it may not be a great position seen by all—rejoice! God will be the one to exalt you, and not man. Rejoice that when God exalts you, it's so much better than the fleeting, wavering, truly unrewarding praise and glory of man. And if you would be quick to despise those of low degree, or over-glorify those people who have exalted statures or ministries, please repent. Remember, it's what God esteems that's important, and often what God esteems is *not* what man esteems.

God is judge. He puts one up and sets down another. He looks not on the outward appearance, but on the heart. How can you know the hearts of men? How do you not know that the same poor man you despised as he pulled into church with a broken car has not given more money to the Lord than the richest of the congregation? Or how do you know if the one serving you by watching your children or cleaning the bathrooms is not someone God has mightily anointed to teach His Word to multitudes one day? You'd greatly honor him if you knew what God was going to be doing in his life. Therefore, honor all men.

Don't treat with contempt any person you feel is not at your level socially, financially, or spiritually. You will sin against God and transgress His commandments: "You shall love your neighbor as yourself" (Matthew 22:39); "Honor everyone" (1 Peter 2:17).

Thank and honor those who serve among you, and especially those who labor in the Word and in doctrine (1 Timothy 5:17). But also thank and honor those who labor unnoticed, unrewarded (in this life), and even unappreciated.

If you serve the Lord, and in your serving, people treat you with contempt—love them! Love them fervently, and love them with a pure heart. Pray diligently for them. Repay evil with good. Honor and serve them all the more faithfully and joyfully, and God will reward you. God will see. Commit yourself to Him that judges righteously, and He will see what you do in His name.

JOY IN THINKING OF WHAT WE HAVE

Deuteronomy 26:11 says, "And you shall rejoice in all the good that the LORD your God has given to you and to your house, you, and the Levite, and the sojourner who is among you." It is right and good that we cheerfully enjoy what God has given to us. Always remember He is the source of all good things. "Every good gift and every perfect gift is from above, coming down from the Father of lights with whom there is no variation or shadow due to change" (James 1:17).

If we've received something good from the Lord, there's no biblical reason to deny ourselves the joy that comes from what we've received. We must, however, always place our adoration for what we've received on the Lord, and let Him be our desire, and not possessions. If your heart is blameless before the Lord, and you have comfortable surroundings, rejoice in them without guilt. John the Baptist said in John 3:27, "A person cannot receive even one thing unless it is given him from heaven."

If you lack what you'd like, be thankful and rejoice in what you do have. Often, how much people think they have relates to their perspective and their level of thankfulness. No matter how many "good things" you have, rejoice in every one of them as you remember it was the Lord your God who gave them to you.

ALWAYS REJOICING

Philippians 4:4 says, "Rejoice in the Lord always; again I will say, Rejoice." What a commandment! On a recent vacation with my family, I determined to keep rejoicing in the Lord no matter how the trip progressed. As I set my heart to rejoice always, it was almost amazing to me how frustrating circumstances could so easily tempt me to go from happily rejoicing in God's goodness to murmuring ungratefully in my heart.

We were staying at a cabin in the local mountains. On one of the days, at about two o'clock in the afternoon, I began getting restless. We hadn't left the cabin all day, so I asked my husband, who was on the couch reading, if we could go do something. He wasn't ready to go out yet, and suddenly I stopped rejoicing. Because I really wanted to go out and didn't get my way, I was tempted to start grumbling in my thoughts.

I didn't say anything to my husband, but I went to a separate bedroom because I needed to examine my heart. I needed the Lord. As I began to pray, I felt like the Lord impressed upon my heart, "You can either obey me and 'Rejoice always, pray without ceasing, give thanks in all circumstances; for this is the will of God in Christ Jesus for you' (1 Thessalonians 5:16-18), or you can complain against Me and be disobedient to Me by your grumbling."

Desiring to please God, I decided to be thankful we were still in the cabin because God knows what is best for us. Then I purposed in my heart to rejoice in Him, both because He is worthy to be rejoiced at continually, and because it is better for me to glorify God by my obedience than to get my way.

During this time, my son came into the room with me. So I said to him, "Let's just pray right now and give God thanks for everything we can think of." We began to thank God and rejoice in Him once more. I'd probably been in the room a total of three minutes when my husband called out to me, saying we could all go do something together after all. So it's possible the whole delay was so I could learn more deeply to really "Rejoice Always"!

If you are in the habit of murmuring or worse when you don't get your way, the Bible commands that instead you are to "Rejoice Always" (1 Thessalonians 5:16), no matter what is happening. Purpose in your heart that no matter what happens in your life, whether or not you get your way in the things you want, you'll still give thanks to God. Part of true reverence of God is rejoicing in Him, because of Him. It's better to glorify God than to have the fleeting happiness of this life by getting what you want.

Rejoicing in the Lord is necessary to experience all the fullness of God. If you want to start rejoicing right at this moment, here is an idea you can begin right now. First, start smiling. Then sing, "Rejoice in the Lord always, and again I say rejoice." You can add dancing with tambourines and gleeful skipping. Some people do cartwheels while smiling incessantly. Of course, if you begin to feel silly or get strange stares, my question is, "Why were you actually doing this in front of people?"

Some of this is silly, but there is a real benefit to worshipping God before only Him and praising Him without reserve. David danced before the Lord with all His might (2 Samuel 6:14), and Paul made mention of a rejoicing he did only before God (2 Corinthians 5:13). Sometimes there is no other way to express heartfelt praise then to do it with outward expressions before the Lord. Be willing to give of yourself to the Lord completely because He is worthy of praise that consumes all of who we are.

~14~

Subtle, Joy Robbing Sins

His divine power has granted to us all things that pertain to life and godliness, through the knowledge of him who called us to his own glory and excellence, by which he has granted to us his precious and very great promises, so that through them you may become partakers of the divine nature, having escaped from the corruption that is in the world because of sinful desire.

2 Peter 1:3-4

Though we've seen how sin in general will keep us from delighting in God, I want us to now examine some specific, subtle but dangerous sins that will severely inhibit happiness in life. These sins are common and often unnoticed. Often we are supremely aware of the "big" sins in our life, or in the lives of others, but we can fail to recognize certain sins that will also rob us of gladness.

If we've climbed far up peaks of joy, but then allow a few pebbles of unbelief or selfishness to dwell securely on our path, soon the mount we've climbed will become a landslide, and our joy will plummet, as it's pulled down by the disastrous weight of iniquity. Only crushed memories of our joy will be left under the magnitude of sin's heaviness. With that in mind, let's consider some of the subtle but major joy sapping sins:

SELFISHNESS AND PRIDE

Can pride really take away joy? The world says it's good to be full of pride and self-confidence, that having pride will make you happy. But though these self-exalting feelings may seem harmless and even beneficial, we have to examine why the Bible says they come before destruction and a fall (Proverbs 16:18).

When the Bible discusses pride (and this is the pride I'm also referring to), it's talking about selfish pride. This pride is the resistance to the will of God and the promotion of our own selves as better than God in our thoughts, plans, or ways. Pride is thinking that in and of ourselves, apart from God, we have something great, something to offer the world, some grounds for doing things our way and not God's way.

And is this thinking even wrong? Yes, because the Bible says that in man, apart from God, dwells no good thing (Romans 7:18). If we therefore have nothing of ourselves to be confident in, satisfaction with ourself is false. This means, thankfully, the only thing we have to glory in is God. "But let him who boasts boast in this, that he understands and knows me, that I am the LORD who practices steadfast love, justice, and righteousness in the earth. For in these things I delight, declares the LORD" (Jeremiah 9:24).

Of the things most sought after in this world, I would say the root of their appeal is they promise glory to the attainer. Consider beauty: The benefit of being beautiful is attention and praise, which is really about receiving honor and glory from people. The same goes for fame. What is the advantage of being famous, except honor and glory from men? This desire to be exalted, to be the greatest in some way, is not uncommon.

Have you ever pursued being the greatest in some way? Did you get jealous over those who were better than you? Or did you achieve your goal? Were you adored and praised because of it?

It's easy for us to want to please people, to yearn for the favor and adoration of others. Think of what accomplishments you want to attain most in life. What is the motive behind your goals? Does it include being recognized by others for something you've done well? Do you desire wealth or beauty or prominence so people will admire you? My prayer for you is that you'll see in this section why pride and self-exaltation are severely dangerous. As we look at what happened to Nebuchadnezzar and Herod because of their pride, I hope you'll shudder in terror at even the thought of being a prideful woman.

During the time the New Testament was written, Herod the king met an untimely death because he allowed himself to receive the praise of man. "On an appointed day Herod put on his royal robes, took his seat upon the throne, and delivered an oration to them. And the people were shouting, 'The voice of a god, and not of a man!' Immediately an angel of the Lord struck him down, because he did not give God the glory, and he was eaten by worms and breathed his last" (Acts 12:21-23).

Much planning must have gone on before this day came. The people had gathered together to hear their great leader speak, and Herod had probably worked hard planning what he would say. Dressed to the hilt and looking good, Herod's moment had arrived. The crowd had gathered, and Herod began to talk. He must have been so pleased when all his efforts were repaid with shouts from the audience: "The voice of a god." What speaker wouldn't want to be adored by his listeners?

Herod soaks up the adoration and makes no mention of God. In his zeal to honor himself, Herod did not give glory to the One to whom glory was due. But God has said, "I am the LORD; that is my name; my glory I give to no other" (Isaiah 42:8). Because Herod received the glory for himself, the angel of the Lord struck him, so that he was eaten of worms and died.

Do you see why it's crucial as godly women that we fiercely guard our hearts from longing after worldly praise, or fame, or power, or riches, or beauty, or anything that this world values and highly esteems? As Christian women it's still very possible to secretly long or strive for these things, but God is serious about the consequences of seeking glory for ourselves.

Another man who desired glory for himself was Nebuchadnezzar. He was a mighty king, but his heart became lifted up with pride. His mind hardened in him, and one day as he was walking through his palace in his kingdom of Babylon, he began to verbally exalt himself, saying, "Is not this great Babylon, which I have built by my mighty power as a royal residence and for the glory of my majesty?" (Daniel 4:30). He praised himself, and gave the glory to himself for the greatness of Babylon. But as the words were still coming out of his mouth, God swiftly brought judgment against him.

In an instant, God removed his kingdom from him and gave him the mind of an animal. His understanding departed from him, and he went to live with the beasts of the field while he ate grass. His hair grew like eagles' feathers and his nails grew like birds' claws (Daniel 4:31-33; 5:18-21). And for seven years God allowed him to live like an animal, until he knew "that the Most High rules the kingdom of men and gives it to whom he will" (Daniel 4:32).

God restored to Nebuchadnezzar his understanding when he learned it's God who gives a man glory, and it's God who can just as swiftly take it away. God gives to whomever He wills power and authority. But it all originates from and with Him, and He alone is worthy to be praised for it.

Thus we must not in any way allow ourselves to receive the glory belonging only to God. Just like Nebuchadnezzar, God can take away a person's mental health as a judgment against the sin of pride. God gives understanding to the person who pleases Him (Ecclesiastes 2:26), but He can also take understanding away as in the case of Nebuchadnezzar. Because Nebuchadnezzar and Herod did not give God the glory that belonged to Him, but desired it for themselves, they instead received shame and abasement.

It is utter wickedness to long after the glory that belongs to God alone. With that said, I believe it's possibly the most common of all sins. By this

I mean, seeking the praise of others is ultimately at the motivating core of many other sins. Now, whether or not I'm right, I do know the temptation of desiring people to recognize, praise, and esteem us is very common: "No temptation has overtaken you that is not common to man" (1 Corinthians 10:13).

It's a temptation I'm sadly familiar with. As a Christian, especially when I was younger, I struggled with desiring outward beauty. This ultimately comes down to a desire for glory.

Physical appearance has been something I've thought much about as a Christian woman, in desiring to learn what is pleasing to God. Apart from modesty, I've learned, for the most part, to draw no conclusions as to the external appearances of others. Yet I do believe a woman should consider her motives concerning her appearance, and let her heart be tender to the conviction of the Holy Spirit so she is pure before the Lord.

A woman should strive in her appearance to please God and her husband, if she is married, since her body belongs to him. Even though I am blessed to have a husband who is very concerned with me dressing modestly, my own heart was not always desirous to be a woman who was completely discreet and chaste (Titus 2:5 KJV). I wanted to dress right over the border: so that I was modest, but just modest enough to still look good. And the issue was really my heart. I didn't want to be plain or terribly out-of-style.

But why would this be an issue? If my looking plain pleased God, than I should have gladly chosen it. The issue was I wanted the approval from people that comes with a pleasing appearance, and I wanted to avoid the rejection that can come with the sometimes "ugly" clothes that are worn to accomplish modesty.

Then one day, as I sat on my bed crying, the Lord worked in my heart a surrender to Him of all the importance I placed on how I looked. I determined to give up being self-conscience about how I looked. I prayed, "Lord, if I am ugly from this day on because I wear baggy clothes, and I am considered plain and ugly, and my clothes are out of style, then that is what I want, God. I do not want to care any more about pleasing people in my appearance except that I might be an example to other women and excel in modesty." I cried because this was one of my worldly influences that I had held most dear, and because I was blessed that God was changing my heart.

After this, when I would get dressed in my "ugly" modest clothing, I would still have to remind myself of why I'd chosen this route. Now I must add, so you don't get the wrong idea, I still do care about my appearance—but I believe God has given me great freedom from wanting to dress in a way that would give me extra attention. I'm still concerned with what I wear, but the focus in my heart has been changed from pleasing people to pleasing God. And let me tell you with as much passion as I can communicate in a book: It has been so freeing!!! Oh, to not obsessively care about my appearance or overly worry about my weight (a benefit of dressing modestly) has been wonderful!

I do believe the Lord even blessed my obedience in modesty by making my weight, to me personally, a non-issue in my life. And that in itself is so freeing! I know, because there was a time in my life while I was a teenager that I was extremely obsessed with my weight and it affected how I saw everything, to the point where I even blamed people's reactions to me on the way I looked. If someone wasn't nice to me, I reasoned that my arms were probably too fat! This is an absolutely silly thought, but one I also know women think.

Now I must add, I'm not advocating that women wear ugly clothes or neglect themselves physically. I did go through a season of wearing "ugly" clothes so that God could strip my heart of the desire to be recognized for my appearance.

But overall, I do care about what I wear. I still have days when I stand in front of my closet, staring at my clothes, and fretting because I doubt anything will look good. I still want to look presentable and appropriate. I still love being able to wear a new outfit. But it's my motive for what I wear that has changed.

So pushing away my sin of seeking recognition in this area has caused me to reap beautiful rewards beyond what I would have expected. One of the most liberating experiences in all the world is having a conscience void of offense towards God and man (Acts 24:16).

If there is an issue in your heart that stands out to you, and you hear the still small voice of God convicting you, don't wait to listen. Seeking for any glory or praise for yourself is pride, and selfishness and pride will sap you of joy. Pride will make you contentious, because Proverbs 13:10 says, "Only by pride cometh contention" (KJV). Pride will remove you far from God's presence, which is the very source of joy. Isaiah 57:15 says,

> For thus says the One who is high and lifted up,
> who inhabits eternity, whose name is Holy:
> "I dwell in the high and holy place,
> and also with him who is of a contrite and lowly spirit,
> to revive the spirit of the lowly,
> and to revive the heart of the contrite."

God dwells with the humble and those who have a contrite spirit. If you're aware of pride in your heart, God's desire is to revive you if you'll repent of your desire for acceptance and the praise of man, and turn to Him with a humble and contrite heart.

DISCONTENTMENT

Like we've just seen, when we're seeking to please ourselves and get our way, we'll be miserable. And when we're not pleased the way we want, we become discontent. Whether our paycheck doesn't have the number we want, the mail doesn't have the letter we want, or our husband won't do the things we want, we show by our discontentment that we don't trust God's ways are perfect and that He has plans for us to give us a future and a hope (Jeremiah 29:11). His plans and ways, including the answers He gives to our prayers (even the "no" answers), are perfect.

How do we know His ways are perfect? Because the Bible declares they are in Deuteronomy 32:4, saying, "He is the Rock, His work is perfect; for all His ways are justice, a God of truth and without injustice; righteous and upright is He" (NKJV). Both 2 Samuel 22:31 and Psalm 18:30 say, "As for God, His way is perfect; the word of the Lord is proven; He is a shield to all who trust in Him" (NKJV). And He makes the way of those that trust in Him perfect also: "God is my strength and power, and He makes my way perfect" (2 Samuel 22:33 NKJV).

Often we aren't content because we're anxious. We believe God is doing a work, but our impatience with His timing causes our frustration and discontentment. Maybe you're not content with where you live, your social life, or your education. Isn't it possible God has allowed these things to be as they are to fulfill the specific plan He has for your life? Since it is possible, be content with where God has you while you earnestly pray for His will, and trust Him.

The Bible gives us the guidelines for contentment in 1 Timothy 6:8, saying, "But if we have food and clothing, with these we will be content." Do you have food and clothing? If you have any clothing at all, or any food, then your answer is yes. Therefore be content.

There are several areas the Bible specifically addresses concerning contentment. The first one I want us to consider is money. Paul instructs Timothy to withdraw himself from anyone who would suppose that gain is godliness (1 Timothy 6:5), and says rather, "Now there is great gain in godliness with contentment" (1 Timothy 6:6).

The love of money is a sin that doesn't discriminate between the rich and the poor. We know from Scripture that the desire for money overtakes both types of people. Those who seek riches are warned by Paul: "But those who desire to be rich fall into temptation, into a snare, into many senseless and harmful desires that plunge people into ruin and destruction. For the love of money is a root of all kinds of evils. It is through this craving that some have wandered away from the faith and pierced themselves with many pangs" (1 Timothy 6:9-10).

In the Proverbs we read that a lazy man can also be just as greedy as those who strive and labor to be rich. Proverbs 21:25-26 says, "The desire of the slothful killeth him; for his hands refuse to labour. He coveteth greedily all the day long: but the righteous giveth and spareth not" (KJV).

God desires us to be content with our financial position as well as our position in the other areas He's placed us. Don't sinfully strive to be in a place God has not placed you. When God desires to exalt you, He will. "Humble yourselves, therefore, under the mighty hand of God so that at the proper time he may exalt you" (1 Peter 5:6). He will exalt you when the time is right, and nothing can stop His hand when He is ready. "For promotion [cometh] neither from the east, nor from the west, nor from the south. But God [is] the judge: he putteth down one, and setteth up another" (Psalms 75:6-7 KJV).

His ways are above our ways, and He will bring what He desires to pass. He is faithful, and we must not ever doubt His faithfulness. Therefore trust Him with a content heart. Don't allow your heart to become consumed with what you don't have, whether you have much or little. Your bones will be sapped of strength and your spirit will be robbed of joy if your heart doesn't rejoice in your portion from God.

God requires us to be content as Christians, and the Bible makes it clear that the call to become a Christian is the call to count all things loss. Philippians 3:8 says, "Indeed, I count everything as loss because of the surpassing worth of knowing Christ Jesus my Lord. For his sake I have suffered the loss of all things and count them as rubbish, in order that I may gain Christ." If we've truly counted all things loss, then anything God gives us will be a great cause of joy and rejoicing to us.

Remember that every good thing we have now is from God. "Every good gift and every perfect gift is from above, coming down from the Father of lights with whom there is no variation or shadow due to change" (James 1:17). The proper mindset of a believer is to have traded all that was once gain for the exceedingly greater treasure of knowing Christ.

Then anything we do get, even necessary food and clothing, will be a great blessing to us.

~15~

More Subtle, Joy Robbing Sins

> *But according to his promise we are waiting for new heavens and a new earth in which righteousness dwells. Therefore, beloved, since you are waiting for these, be diligent to be found by him without spot or blemish, and at peace.*
>
> *2 Peter 3:13-14*

*I*n the last chapter we explored pride and discontentment, two perilously widespread sins. It's easy to downplay the seriousness of these transgressions, but their hair-raising consequences can't be overlooked.

In this chapter we'll look at three more "minor" sins with severe penalties. I ask you to really search your heart and see if you're trapped under the weight of any of these iniquities. Pray God would free you from their stronghold and give you grace to overcome temptation. Pray for God to engulf your heart with desire to please Him.

INGRATITUDE

And what a sin this is! There's not much difference between discontentment and ingratitude, and when one is present, the other is usually also found. But ingratitude can be so easily cured by simply giving thanks. The Bible commands us to always be thankful: "In every thing give thanks: for this is the will of God in Christ Jesus concerning you" (1 Thessalonians 5:18 KJV). It can be hard to always remember to give thanks in everything, but this is God's will for your life.

Can you think of a way that would make it easier to remember to continually express your gratitude to God? Even something as simple as wearing a special bracelet can remind you throughout the day to be appreciative toward God for everything. Consider how much your level of joy would improve if you were constantly thanking God from a truly appreciative heart.

What a blessing it is to recognize that everything we have is from God's hand. If you haven't been faithfully giving God thanks in everything, take a moment to confess this sin to God and begin to be grateful in every circumstance.

UNBELIEF

As I consider the sin of unbelief, I think of the children of Israel, and how, when they were wandering in the wilderness, God decided they'd stay there until they died. What made God so angry that He decided they'd *never* enter the Promised Land, but only see it from a distance? What wickedness happened on that "day of temptation in the wilderness" (Psalm 95:8) to make God give this final word? Something so terrible occurred that God was ready to destroy all the Israelites except Moses (Numbers 14:12).

The Bible teaches us that before this day of temptation, the children of Israel had complained repeatedly, and this murmuring had displeased the Lord. They'd murmured against God for lack of meat, and, at times, water. But their murmuring had its roots in something even deeper, and that was their unbelief of God.

In the events leading up to their day of temptation, the children of Israel were wandering in the wilderness, and they had begun to tell Moses to send spies into the land that God had promised would become theirs (Deuteronomy 1:22-23). Numbers 13:1 also says that God spoke to Moses to send men to spy out the land of Canaan, so the men must first have approached Moses, with God afterward confirming men be sent out to spy out the land. Twelve men were chosen to go, one from each tribe.

Then before they even set one foot in the promised land, to spy it out, God told them, "Send men to spy out the land of Canaan, *which I am giving to the people of Israel*" (Numbers 13:2, italics added). God had already told the children of Israel the land was theirs. After spending forty days spying out the land God had promised them, the twelve spies returned to the children of Israel with their report.

They acknowledged the land was a good land, but then ten of the spies begin to discourage the Israelites. They said the men of the land were giants who were stronger than them, and that those men would win against them in battle. (The complete story can be found in Numbers 13-14.)

The day these words were spoken was the day Hebrews 3:8 refers to as the "day of testing in the wilderness." The Israelites were being tempted with a choice: Believe God or believe the report of these ten spies.

They could have chosen to believe God would give them the land as He'd promised. After all, He was the God who'd done wonders before them, who led them by a pillar of fire by night and a cloudy pillar by day, and gave them manna to eat every morning. But they refused to believe. They instead replied against the Lord, saying, "Why is the LORD bringing us into this land, to fall by the sword? Our wives and our little ones will become a prey. Would it not be better for us to go back to Egypt?" (Numbers 14:3).

On their day of temptation, when they could have believed the land would be theirs, they failed by refusing to believe God's word. Instead they believed the ten wicked spies who said God would not give them the land, but the land would instead swallow them up and they'd die in it. God told them the land would be theirs, but they believed the land would consume them. God had already said He'd given the land to the children of Israel, and they refused to believe!

Psalm 106:24-25 says, "Then they despised the pleasant land, having no faith in his promise. They murmured in their tents, and did not obey the voice of the LORD." Their murmuring was the outpouring of their unbelieving hearts. Hebrews 3:18 says, "And to whom sware he that they should not enter into his rest, but to them that believed not?" (KJV). Because they did not believe God, they were filled with murmurings against Him.

God responds with severe judgment against them for their unbelief: Every single person in the wilderness from twenty years old and older would die, and never enter the Promised Land, except Caleb and Joshua, who were the two spies who did believe God. This story and the warning in it are not for the Israelites alone. Hebrews 3:12 warns us to also take heed to ourselves, so that there is not in us an evil heart of unbelief like the Israelites, in departing from the living God.

We are never to consider our own unbelief as excusable, but we must condemn unbelief in ourselves as a great sin. C. H. Spurgeon said,

> It is a very easy thing for us to get into a desponding state of heart, and to mistrust the promises and faithfulness of God [...] It will be far wiser for each one of us to feel, This unbelief of mine is a great wrong in the sight of God. He has never given me any occasion for it, and I am doing him a cruel injustice by thus doubting him. I must not idly sit down, and say, "This has come upon me like a fever, or a paralysis, which I cannot help;" but I must rather say, "This is a great sin, in which I must no longer indulge; but I must confess my unbelief, with shame and self-abasement, to think that there should be in me this evil heart of unbelief.[1]"

Part of what makes our unbelief in God so distressing is how often we've seen firsthand His faithfulness. I think of my own life and how many times God has shown me His goodness and His power. Because I've seen the workings of God, any unbelief I have is all the more unbelievable, and the wickedness of my unbelief all the more wicked.

Say you owned a business, and you had a favorite employee you wouldn't trade for anything. Because she was valuable to you, it was your priority to make sure she knew you'd never fire her; on the contrary, you often reassured her of her job security and treated her with great love and kindness, doing whatever was possible to keep her happy. Imagine how you'd feel if, after years of your expressing how indispensable she was to you, she suddenly quit because she feared being fired. She doubted you liked her, and mistrusted her job security. That would probably cause you great soreness of emotion, for all you'd done was not recognized because of her unbelief.

Even still, as sinners we can have a valid unbelief of one another. But with God there can be no valid unbelief. He is perfect, faithful, and all powerful. We can trust Him because He has promised to work all things together for good (Romans 8:28).

Unbelief of God is all the more painful because God is altogether believable. He is faithful. "If we believe not, [yet] he abideth faithful: he cannot deny himself" (2 Timothy 2:13 KJV). If we do not force ourselves to believe God's Word completely, we will not be able to experience the fullness of joy God has made available for us. Romans 15:13 shows us it is through believing that God fills us with joy and peace: "May the God of hope fill you with all joy and peace in believing, so that by the power of the Holy Spirit you may abound in hope."

FEAR AND ANXIETY

I've read that in the United States there are more than nineteen million people who have extreme anxiety or anxiety attacks. Even in the church of God, multitudes of people experience anxiety as part of their lives. But anxiety is the result of unbelief. If we look at Matthew 6:25, Jesus instructs us to not be anxious about our lives, referring to what we eat, drink, and wear. Then three more times, in verses 27, 31, and 34, Jesus addresses anxiety again, saying we're not to be anxious. So anxiety is a sin God commands us against.

Anxiety can't be blamed on heredity, because sin itself is hereditary. I do believe it's possible a woman's personality type or upbringing may affect her, so that anxiety comes more naturally to her, but we have all inherited a sinful nature from Adam. A propensity toward anxiety may make dealing with it more difficult, but God still requires anxiety to be dealt with in the same way we would deal with the sins of unbelief, unthankfulness, stealing, jealously, bitterness, etc. Philippians 4:6 says, "Do not be anxious about anything, but in everything by prayer and supplication with thanksgiving let your requests be made known to God." Which means, be anxious about nothing!

This is why it's so important we don't blame our anxiety on genetics: because there's no cure if anxiety is genetic. But when we recognize anxiety is rooted in sinful fear, there can be repentance leading to freedom. Every person has experienced fear, and I believe anxiety and fear are extremely common among women.

We can all relate to anxiety and/or fear on some level. Can you think of a situation that has occurred, or repeatedly occurs, where you are likely to experience fear and/or anxiety? (If nothing comes to mind, try sharing your faith in Christ with strangers and neighbors more often. Or else, congratulations on your boldness!) If a situation has come to your mind, imagine yourself in that circumstance without any fear or anxiety, and imagine yourself filled with faith, completely trusting in God during that time. What would that situation be like? How would you feel instead of fearful?

Instead of fear there would be calm. And this is what God desires for you. The Bible says, "There is no fear in love, but perfect love casts out fear. For fear has to do with punishment, and whoever fears has not been perfected in love" (1 John 4:18). It is tormenting to be afraid of things. We may fear people, circumstances, or suffering, but the Bible cautions us to not fear any of these things.

I want us to explore together the biblical answers to combat each of these fears. First, let's observe what the Bible says about not fearing people. We're warned by Jesus against the fear of man in Luke 12:4-5. He says, "I tell you, my friends, do not fear those who kill the body, and after that have nothing more that they can do. But I will warn you whom to fear: fear him who, after he has killed, has authority to cast into hell. Yes, I tell you, fear him!"

Hebrews 13:6 also reiterates this thought, saying "So that we may boldly say, The Lord [is] my helper, and I will not fear what man shall do unto me" (KJV). There is no fear in death when we know the living God, and so we don't need to be afraid of those who can only kill us physically.

Along with not fearing man, we understand through Christ's exhortation to the church at Ephesus that we are not to fear suffering. Revelation 2:10 says, "Do not fear what you are about to suffer." This statement to the church at Ephesus was followed by a prophecy that they were going to be thrown into prison and then tortured for ten days before dying: "Behold, the devil is about to throw some of you into prison, that you may be tested, and for ten days you will have tribulation. Be faithful unto death, and I will give you the crown of life" (Revelation 2:10).

These would be heavy words to hear. Yet if the Ephesians were admonished to not even be afraid of torture and death, then we can take heart to not be afraid of things that are much less significant. God will strengthen you to have a sound mind if you will put your confidence in Him. Second Timothy 1:7 says, "For God hath not given us the spirit of fear; but of power, and of love, and of a sound mind" (KJV).

Lastly, we must not fear circumstances. Psalm 46:1-3 says,

> God is our refuge and strength,
> a very present help in trouble.
> Therefore we will not fear though the earth gives way,
> though the mountains be moved into the heart of the sea,

> though its waters roar and foam,
> though the mountains tremble at its swelling. *Selah*.

Even if the mountains were being tossed into the oceans through strong natural disasters, God will still be our very near help, and we must trust Him without fear.

David boldly proclaimed, "Though an army encamp against me, my heart shall not fear; though war arise against me, yet I will be confident" (Psalm 27:3). Circumstances will change throughout life, but our confidence in the Lord must be so secure that we agree with David that our hearts will not fear.

If there's something you avoid doing because of fear, but the Bible is clear God has called you to do it, pray God would strengthen you to fear nothing but Him. Pray a prayer of confession to God, and ask Him to help you not be anxious. Now choose to be confident in the Lord. Anxious, fearful thoughts must be replaced with a heart that obeys God, completely and confidently trusting in Him.

Anxiety is a sin that will utterly and entirely rob you of joy. The symptoms of anxiety include panic attacks, difficulty breathing, nausea, constipation, diarrhea, stomach upset, difficulty concentrating, negative thoughts, and even fear of normal activities—and this list is not inclusive. None of these symptoms are pleasant, and some are worse than others.

If you experience any of these things because of anxiety, be hopeful, because God is the cure to anxiety. He knows us perfectly and intimately, and He has given us a practical solution that works! Diligently following these easy and viable steps from the Bible will prove to be overwhelmingly worth the effort.

Philippians 4:6-7 says, "Have no anxiety about anything, but in everything by prayer and supplication with thanksgiving let your requests be made known to God. And the peace of God, which passes all understanding, will keep your hearts and your minds in Christ Jesus" (RSV). The first five words are a commandment: Have no anxiety about anything. As redundant as it sounds, in order to not have anxiety you must choose to stop being anxious. Replace anxiety with prayer, supplication, and thanksgiving. When these three things have filled your heart, God will give you His peace, which is beyond understanding, and it will guard your heart and your mind in Christ Jesus.

This is how I personally apply this verse to my life: When I feel anxious about a situation, I first begin my prayer by recognizing the greatness of God and His complete power and control of all things. Often I will write out my prayer in a journal, and I have found that for me this is very effective, though God knows all our thoughts and so to Him a journal is not necessary. (But I still personally encourage journaling.)

Then I explain my situation to Him. I know He already knows the situation, but to explain it helps me by getting it off my chest. I don't always write *everything* in the journal, but like David, I try to pour out my own feelings before the Lord.

While journaling, I pray about what I would like God to do. I pray very idealistically. I pray specifically and exactly for what I'd like to happen if I were the one who could change it. I do this because James 4:2 says, "You do not have, because you do not ask." I don't want to not have something because I didn't ask. So I (usually) ask the Lord for specifically what I would desire.

Then I must say, "Nevertheless, not my will, but yours, be done" (Luke 22:42). My own desires may be the opposite of what God knows is best, and often I want something one day and praise Him the next day that I didn't receive it. James 4:3 says, "You ask and do not receive, because you ask wrongly, to spend it on your passions."

I know if my prayer is not what pleases God, then God will be faithful to see that I don't receive what I've asked amiss. And I'm very thankful for this, because God knows what I need perfectly. Then I turn my thoughts to thank God. I thank Him for everything about the situation I've just prayed about. I thank Him for who He is. I thank Him that I can cast all my cares upon Him, because He cares for me. I thank Him for everything I can think of that I have to be thankful for.

And do you know what happens next? My heart *is* filled with peace. And it does transcend all understanding. I'm able to hope completely in my God. I remember how God has *always* been faithful to me, and so I am confident that He will be faithful still.

TURNING FROM SIN

Consider right now with me if you have been able to identify with committing any of the sins discussed in this chapter or the previous one. If you recognize that you've transgressed in one or more of these areas, then please come back with me to Psalm 38 where David confesses his sin with sorrow. He says in verses 17-18, "For I am ready to fall, and my pain is ever before me. I confess my iniquity; I am sorry for my sin."

Confessing our sin to God is so good for us, especially because it keeps us from being as easily deceived by the same sin again. We vocalize our sins to God so we can agree and even discuss with God why our sin was wrong. It's important in repentance, especially in those sins prone to be repeated, that people examine the Scriptures concerning their errors, and confess their faults to God with humility, asking for forgiveness and cleansing of the sin. Allow yourself to feel the godly sorrow that is a result of your sin. Don't justify any sin, but agree with God, calling sin what it is, and confessing it to Him. Don't sin by not believing God's Word concerning sin.

Then know, "If we confess our sins, he is faithful and just to forgive us our sins and to cleanse us from all unrighteousness" (1 John 1:9). This is speaking to believers, who have already put their faith in Jesus and had His righteousness imputed to them. God will cleanse us from unrighteousness in the same physical sense that the sins were committed, juxtaposed with the cleansing from unrighteousness in the spiritual sense at salvation. Often our mind *needs* a good cleansing after we've sinned! Now believe that through Jesus, God has removed your sin as far as the east is from the west. Believing this will be the escape from the guilt-bred misery and destruction of self-pity.

When we become aware of our sins as we commit them, let's examine ourselves. Then, confessing our sin, we must agree with God about the sinfulness of our actions so we'll no longer be held captive by sin, but free and clean, ready for righteousness and obedience in the inward parts, and motivated by ardor and passion for the very God who redeemed us from all iniquity and set us apart for good works.

~16~

Examples of Joy

To this end we always pray for you, that our God may make you worthy of his calling and may fulfill every resolve for good and every work of faith by his power, so that the name of our Lord Jesus may be glorified in you, and you in him, according to the grace of our God and the Lord Jesus Christ.
2 Thessalonians 1:11-12

$\mathcal{A}$s we conclude this book, I want to say how blessed I am you've continued with me until now. My prayer is that God has brought you to a place of deeper and more steadfast joy in Him. I hope you've been able to receive with gladness all that the Bible says concerning what God requires of us emotionally. I hope you've become as excited as I am over the riches we have as children of God, and that "you are not lacking in any spiritual gift, as you wait for the revealing of our Lord Jesus Christ, who will sustain you to the end, guiltless in the day of our Lord Jesus Christ" (1 Corinthians 1:7-8). I would even like to say thank you because I am so thankful that you have come to this place with me: So thank you.

Now as we prepare to conclude our journey, the last thing I would like us to do together is ponder the examples of David, Paul, and Jesus. One of the terrific blessings of studying the Bible is learning about people who have lived before us in ways pleasing to God. Having gone before us, these saints are now examples for us to follow. Hebrews 6:12 exhorts us to "not be sluggish, but imitators of those who through faith and patience inherit the promises." Those who have inherited the promises are the saints who have died in the Lord before us. We must attentively imitate their example of faith in God and their patience in waiting for His fulfillment of the promises.

Again, in James 5:10-11, we are exhorted to follow the prophets as they are examples to us: "As an example of suffering and patience, brethren, take the prophets who spoke in the name of the Lord. Behold, we call those happy who were steadfast. You have heard of the steadfastness of Job, and you have seen the purpose of the Lord, how the Lord is compassionate and merciful" (RSV). As we study those saints who have endured much, while knowing their end is glory, we count them happy. They endured much suffering and affliction while on earth, but now they have been glorified, and so they are surely rejoicing. Their end is joy, the fulfillment of God's promises, and glory.

And enduring is something that the longer you endure, the more you are actually enduring. Patience and enduring speak of trials that can last a long time. Yet, it's our obligation to follow the biblical examples of patience through suffering, because we've also seen the mercy of God through their lives, and that God is very good, and it is always well in the end for those who trust in Him.

DAVID

One of those examples is David, who grew up as a shepherd boy to become king of all Israel and Judah. Many of the Psalms I've quoted were written by him and a large portion of the Bible is dedicated to the story of his life. I want us to look at a few significant events and David's reaction in them.

The story of David begins in 1 Samuel 16. The prophet Samuel is given instructions by God to anoint the next king of Israel. He will be one of the sons of Jesse the Bethlehemite. For Samuel to anoint one of Jesse's sons to be king meant that neither the current King Saul nor any of his sons would rule after him. Samuel realized that if King Saul knew what he was doing, Saul would want to kill him.

So Samuel went to Bethlehem under the pretext that he was going to sacrifice to the Lord. He sent word to Jesse to bring his sons to the sacrifice. When Samuel arrived, all of Jesse's sons were waiting there except David. David was the youngest son, and he hadn't been invited to the sacrifice with his brothers. Instead he was out shepherding the sheep.

As each of David's brothers passed before Samuel, the Lord spoke to Samuel that He had not chosen any of them. Samuel asked if there was anyone else, and Jesse told him of David. David was then called to come, and as Samuel saw him, the Lord said to Samuel, "'Arise, anoint him, for this is he.' Then Samuel took the horn of oil and anointed him in the midst of his brothers. And the Spirit of the LORD rushed upon David from that day forward" (1 Samuel 16:12-13). Estimates of David's age at the time of his anointing range from ten to fifteen years old, so David was still young at this time.

This event catapulted David into more excitement and adventure then he'd probably ever imagined. After David's anointing, Saul began to be troubled by an evil spirit. Saul was told that David was skilled in playing music, so David was called to go to king Saul and there play music for him. Imagine spending your days taking care of sheep and meditating on the Lord, when suddenly you're anointed the next king. Then you're summoned to play music before the present king, and you become immersed in learning the activities of kingly life.

Soon after, you volunteer to go fight a huge Philistine giant, and King Saul agrees to let you. You trust that God will certainly be with you to defeat Goliath, because he dared to speak against the living God, and you're right. You win!

Then the women begin to sing songs about how Saul has killed his thousands, but *you* have killed your ten thousands. It feels great to receive so much praise, but when you're back with King Saul to play your music, he throws a javelin at you in an attempt to kill you. His jealousy of you drives him mad and you must run for your life! Suddenly your entire life has changed.

This is exactly what happened to David. Saul became so jealous of David that he began to mindlessly pursue him with the intent to kill. Through it all, David still put his confidence in the Lord. Let me summarize briefly the the next few major events in David's life.

David became very close friends with Saul's son, Jonathan. Still, Saul wanted David dead, and David stayed in hiding to escape Saul's madness. Saul had been anointed by the Lord when he became king, and for that reason David would not lay even one hand upon him or defend himself against Saul. Instead the brave and victorious David stayed concealed as he fled from place to place.

As David was running, he was given refuge by Achish, a Philistine king of Gath. But Achish's servants told him about David's victory over Goliath. David became very afraid of Achish, and he began to feign lunacy while in front of him. David even let drool run down his beard. Here was the future king of Israel with a Philistine king, scared for his life, and drooling no less! He had gone from being a simple shepherd, to a great hero, to a fugitive pretending to be insane! Achish wanted nothing to do with this crazy escapee of Israel, and so let him go.

Immediately after, David found refuge in a cave at Adullam. It was while David was at Adullam that he wrote Psalm 57. In Psalm 57:1-2, David begins his prayer to the Lord, saying, "Be merciful to me, O God, be merciful to me, for in you my soul takes refuge; in the shadow of your wings I will take refuge, till the storms of destruction pass by. I cry out to God Most High, to God who fulfills his purpose for me." Distressed by constantly running from his enemies to save his life, David still knew whom he should call upon in his anguish.

He cried out to the Lord, and as he did, his psalm of deliverance became a psalm of worship. Look at how David is able to praise God even as he is hiding from a crazed king, in a country where most of the citizens are loyal to that king, and after just having spent time faking mental illness before another king! Those circumstances would probably cause many a strong man to crumble. But instead of crumbling, David became even stronger because he fixed his heart upon the Lord.

He says at the end of the Psalm he wrote while in the cave:

> My heart is steadfast, O God,
> my heart is steadfast!
> I will sing and make melody!
> Awake, my glory!
> Awake, O harp and lyre!
> I will awake the dawn!
> I will give thanks to you, O Lord, among the peoples;
> I will sing praises to you among the nations.
> For your steadfast love is great to the heavens,
> your faithfulness to the clouds.
> Be exalted, O God, above the heavens!
> Let your glory be over all the earth!
> (Psalm 57:7-11)

Would you expect, after all David has gone through, for him to want to tell everyone about God's faithfulness? We may expect him to be discouraged that he hasn't become king, and it wouldn't have seemed unusual if David even complained a bit for having to stay hidden in a cave. But instead of finding fault with God, David praises Him! He's not seeking to be exalted as king. He's asking God to be exalted!

Now let's skip forward a bit in David's life. After spending years waiting to be king, the time finally arrived. Saul died in a battle, and the elders of Judah anointed David as king. It's estimated David spent between fifteen and twenty years waiting before he became king of Judah. I think it's very possible there will be promises of God in our lives we may also have to wait twenty years to see fulfilled, and sometimes even longer.

Don't be surprised by having to wait. If David had spent his time complaining about the wait, it's possible he would not have been the man God described as being after His own heart (1 Samuel 13:14). Instead his meditation was, "Wait for the LORD; be strong, and let your heart take courage; wait for the LORD!" (Psalm 27:14). So after many years of waiting and learning, the time came when the elders of Judah anointed him as king.

Some years later David also became king of Israel, and up to this point David had enjoyed a successful reign. Second Samuel 11:2-12:15 tells the next story about David that I want us to see. One evening when David's armies were out at war, he took a walk on the roof of his house and saw a beautiful woman taking a bath on her house. David had the woman brought to him, though she was married, and he slept with her. She became pregnant, and after failing to make her own husband sleep with her, David finally ordered her husband killed.

After her husband died, David took the woman, named Bathsheba, to be his wife. And you would think after committing the colossal sins of adultery and murder, David would have been sorry. Instead he was oblivious.

It took God sending Nathan the prophet to tell David a parable for David to realize what he'd done. But when he did at last understand how deep his error was, he repented greatly. It was at this time in David's life that he wrote Psalms 32 and 51. There is so much more that can be told about David and his life, but I want to conclude this section by focusing on Psalm 32, in light of the reasons why David first penned this psalm.

David was not writing this psalm with an attitude of self-pity because he had to suffer consequences for his sins. Instead he began by acknowledging that God's forgiveness meant God counted David as never having even committed iniquity. Psalm 32:1-2 says, "Blessed is the one whose transgression is forgiven, whose sin is covered. Blessed is the man against whom the LORD counts no iniquity, and in whose spirit there is no deceit." He was referring to himself even though he had committed adultery and ordered an innocent man killed! He declared himself blessed because God had removed his sin.

He next talks about the distress of his sin in verses 3-4, saying, "For when I kept silent, my bones wasted away through my groaning all day long. For day and night your hand was heavy upon me; my strength was dried up as by the heat of summer. *Selah.*" When sin is unacknowledged, a woman's conscience becomes burdened, whether she sees it or not.

Often a woman who won't turn from her sin and hardens her heart will ease the pressure by focusing on something else. She'll take great measures to ignore the conviction of God's Spirit. The injury of sin will worsen until it becomes unbearably anguishing, like a sore that is left untended until the wound is so infected that the pain becomes consuming. But everything she does to diminish the guilt will be ineffective until she refreshes her soul in times of true confession and repentance in the presence of the Lord.

David said the pressure of his sin was so great that his bones wasted away. He became physically weak until he confessed his sin. Then he found rest in the Lord: "I acknowledged my sin to you, and I did not cover my iniquity; I said, 'I will confess my transgressions to the LORD,' and you forgave the iniquity of my sin. *Selah*" (Psalm 32:5).

After describing his affliction from his sin, and confessing, David begins to do something so uncommon. He begins to rejoice! What a picture for us. Our sin must be taken very seriously, but once we've repented, there's no need to work our way back into God's favor. We're already in God's favor because of Jesus Christ. Regardless of how deeply we've sinned, it's possible for us to be so happy after repentance we shout for joy because Jesus Christ endured the punishment we deserved. See how greatly David rejoiced even though his sin was tremendous: "Many are the sorrows of the wicked, but steadfast love surrounds the one who trusts in the LORD. Be glad in the LORD, and rejoice, O righteous, and shout for joy, all you upright in heart!" (Psalm 32:10).

Even after failure, it's possible to be so caught up in gladness we might shout for joy. Even though we'll still sin, a woman who continually returns to the Lord as her refuge will be surrounded with steadfast love, and she will find Him to be the happiest place on earth. Never is the grace of God to be used for lasciviousness, but because even when we sin, God is still gracious, there is reason to rejoice. "But now that you have been set free from sin and have become slaves of God, the fruit you get leads to sanctification and its end, eternal life" (Romans 6:22).

PAUL

Another example of a saint who lived his life joyfully and pleasing to God is Paul. We learn much about him in the New Testament through both the book of Acts and his own letters written to various churches. Paul endured many hardships as a disciple of Jesus, and for His name's sake he was beaten, imprisoned, and cruelly tortured. Yet this same man was the author who said, "Rejoice in the Lord always; again I will say, Rejoice" (Philippians 4:4).

Paul's life and example of both serving the Lord without reserve and rejoicing with great joy in the midst of his suffering can be a strong source of encouragement to us, if we will follow his steps. His own exhortation is that we would do just that. He said, "I urge you, then, be imitators of me" (1 Corinthians 4:16). In writing to the Philippians he said, "Brothers, join in imitating me, and keep your eyes on those who walk according to the example you have in us" (Philippians 3:17). The events of his life and his sufferings are recorded as patterns for us to follow.

The parts of his life documented in the book of Acts reveal glimpses of his godly character as an example to us. In Acts 20, as Paul is hastening toward Jerusalem, he sends for the elders of the church at Ephesus to come to him at Miletus. When they arrive, Paul tells them he knows he will be bound in Jerusalem, but that he's not moved by it. "None of these things move me, neither count I my life dear unto myself, so that I might finish my course with joy, and the ministry, which I have received of the Lord Jesus, to testify the gospel of the grace of God" (Acts 20:24 KJV).

Paul's primary objective in not being moved by his circumstances was to finish his course with joy. His course was the course of his life, and his aim in life was to finish with joy, and be faithful to testify of the gospel of the grace of God. Paul wanted to obey God by his rejoicing no matter what his life experiences were to actually be.

No matter what the course of our life may be or might have been, God has called us to rejoice in Him so we might both finish our own course with joy and be faithful witnesses of the gospel of the grace of God. In not considering our lives as precious, we can be freed up to truly rejoice in the Lord. When we're troubled and distressed by our offenses and trials, so that we lose our joy, there needs to be a counting of our own lives as not dear unto ourselves (Acts 20:24). Take up this exhortation to not value your goals as greater than pleasing God so you might finish your course of life with great rejoicing! Count and reckon all things as loss to win Christ.

When the believers did just that, Paul encouraged them, saying, "And you became imitators of us and of the Lord, for you received the word in much affliction, with the joy of the Holy Spirit" (1 Thessalonians 1:6). Although they were afflicted, they still rejoiced by the power of the Holy Spirit. Be a follower of Paul, so that no matter the degree of your affliction, you can receive God's words with joy and rejoice in the Lord by the power of the Holy Spirit.

JESUS

Ah, the one whose name is above all names, who came to earth as God in human flesh and lived in absolute sinlessness. He is our ultimate example. Paul said the reason he (Paul) should be an example to us was that he also followed Christ. "Be imitators of me, as I am of Christ" (1 Corinthians 11:1). The examples we have of Jesus, Paul, and David, are not just examples of joy, but they are examples of great joy while in the midst of tremendous suffering. We follow Jesus in both joy and in suffering. As we suffer persecution for following Christ (2 Timothy 3:12), we are still called to both rejoice and be blameless. This example set by Jesus is explained in 1 Peter 2:21-24:

> For to this you have been called, because Christ also suffered for you, leaving you an example, so that you might follow in his steps. He committed no sin, neither was deceit found in his mouth. When he was reviled, he did not revile in return; when he suffered, he did not threaten, but continued entrusting himself to him who judges justly. He himself bore our sins in his body on the tree, that we might die to sin and live to righteousness. By his wounds you have been healed.

We are called to this very thing, to suffer even as Christ suffered. When Jesus called Paul to be a disciple, He said to him in Acts 9:16, "For I will show him how much he must suffer for the sake of my name." Paul passed on to us this same calling. He wrote in Philippians 1:29, "For it has been granted to you that for the sake of Christ you should not only believe in him but also suffer for his sake." If you are a Christian today, it has been given to you on the behalf of Christ to suffer for His sake. "Indeed, all who desire to live a godly life in Christ Jesus will be persecuted" (2 Timothy 3:12). Receive this as gain, because in partaking in the sufferings of Christ you will know Him more (Philippians 3:10).

Not partaking in the sufferings of Christ is like being born without the sense of smell. Although you will not know exactly what you are missing, something very significant will be lacking in your life that can never be explained to the same degree of the experience. Suffering causes us to know Christ through His suffering.

Then, as we are to follow His example of blameless suffering, we are also to follow the example of Christ's joy. Hebrews 12:2 says, "Looking to Jesus, the founder and perfecter of our faith, who for the joy that was set before him endured the cross, despising the shame, and is seated at the right hand of the throne of God." We must fix our eyes on Jesus, who endured the cross because of the joy set before Him. We also have great joy set before us as we endure the trials of this life. Our joy is in seeing

Examples of Joy

Christ's face and His glory, and all the blessings that await us in the ages to come.

Because we will be soon receiving the end of our faith, which is the salvation of our souls (1 Peter 1:9), we also like Christ endure because of that joy set before us. If there was ever one who had an excuse to not rejoice, it would be Christ. He knew the world would mostly reject Him, crucify Him, that He'd be betrayed by a close friend and denied by one of His very closest friends. He knew He'd endure a shameful and excruciatingly painful crucifixion while being publicly mocked and accused of crimes He never committed. Yet while He knew what He was going to suffer, He also knew He'd come from eternal glory with His Father, and that He was God.

Think about this. Jesus knew He was God and yet would endure agonizing sufferings. He who is alone worthy of glory knew that He would be shamed to a degree most of us cannot even imagine. If there was ever a reason to complain or not rejoice, this would be it. So if Christ could rejoice through all this, how much more should we rejoice in our suffering?

And Christ did not mildly rejoice, but His joy exceeded the joy of all other men. Hebrews 1:9 says, "You have loved righteousness and hated wickedness; therefore God, your God, has anointed you with the oil of gladness beyond your companions." Jesus Christ was anointed with more joy and gladness than all His friends and acquaintances. His joy reached the peaks of joy. My prayer for you and me is that we might wholeheartedly imitate Christ, love Him, and fellowship in His joy as we long for the day we'll see Him.

REJOICING WITH INEXPRESSIBLE JOY

One of my very closest and dearest friends, Nicole, who was my maid of honor in my wedding, has for many years wanted a big family. After having a boy and a girl, she easily became pregnant with her third child.

During her first routine ultrasound, the doctor told her that something didn't look right with her baby. She would need a second ultrasound with a specialist. At the next ultrasound, it was confirmed that her baby had a congenital heart defect. Though her own heart was broken that something was wrong with her baby, she was told there was a good chance he would be fine.

Her son, Jaiven Richard, was born seven days early at the beginning of January. He had to stay in the hospital for his first week. But as soon as he was strong enough to nurse on his own, Nicole and her husband Mike were able to take him home. The next week at home with their new baby was precious. Nicole spent many hours nursing, cuddling, and loving her precious newborn. But by the end of the week, something was wrong. He started turning blue and struggled to breath. They quickly called an ambulance and rode with their baby to the hospital.

As the weeks turned into months, and when things seemed like they couldn't get any worse—they did. Her husband was out of work for six weeks and Nicole had to begin working. The children's hospital that her son was in was almost an hour away, but she faithfully visited her son every day to see him and nurse him. She was exhausted and overwhelmed, but she kept going. At the hospital, the doctors and nurses always seemed hopeful.

Jaiven had to undergo an intense open heart surgery and a partial heart transplant. During this time, scriptures about suffering and trusting in God became very real to Nicole. When she felt God impressing the question: "Are you going to trust me with this?" on her heart, she said, "Yes Lord. You're the author and giver of life. You appoint man's days and You hold each person's breath in Your hands. So what can I say? How can I reply against You Lord?"

After the surgery, her son recovered successfully, but then he got the E.coli bacteria. And again he recovered. Throughout it all, Nicole made a solid resolve every time she saw her son to say "God is sovereign." She knew there was a reason why she was suffering as a Christian. The suffering wasn't a punishment—it was for the glory of God.

Next, Jaiven got sick with a cold, but even with his immune deficiency, he again successfully recovered. The roller coaster they had been on became even shakier and he developed chronic lung disease. Jaiven's organs began shutting down and his body became so swollen that his ears couldn't even be seen.

How God was being glorified began to be revealed to them during this time. Though Nicole felt like she was falling apart, the hospital staff was astonished by Mike and Nicole's example. As they began to build relationships with the nurses and doctors, many of the employees began to comment on how differently they were responding to their child dying. The nurses would say to Mike and Nicole, "We're all so amazed that you're still with your family. So many couples at this point are divorced."

Their son was in the part of the children's hospital where every child has a heart condition. Because of the intense grief and pressure the parents in these situations are under, each family is assigned a social worker. When their social worker said to them "Tell me, what is keeping you going? You're amazing me." All they could say was, "It's the Lord." God always gave them the strength at the moment they needed it. God gave them strength to believe what He said.

On a Tuesday, when their son was six months old, they were finally told that there was nothing else the doctors could do. He was going to die. The weather in Colorado was warm and sunny. Nicole petitioned the hospital for the chance to take her son outside. That Thursday the request was partially granted, and Mike and Nicole were able to take their son to a private room with a balcony.

They brought a small stereo to the hospital and set it up in the room. With worship music playing, they took their son out onto the balcony and let him feel the warm, fresh air. Knowing he was going to die soon, they held him there in the sunshine and sang worship music over him.

The next day, as their six-month old son lay across both Nicole and Mike's lap, he passed away. Nicole broke down crying, trusting that God had allowed her son to live, though God knew he would die. With her heart awakened to God's goodness, even in the midst of heart wrenching grief, she prayed, "Please be glorified through my son's death." Nicole didn't necessarily understand everything that God was doing through her tragedy, but she was willing to honor God even when she couldn't understand.

There may be things in your life you don't understand. Are you willing to say in those times, "Lord, be glorified"? If your pursuit in life is to be comfortable, to exalt yourself and be preserved from embarrassment and pain, every trial will only make you more miserable.

But if you've determined that what you want more than anything else in the world is to glorify God, you'll be able to accept whatever happens in your live as being for good, knowing God is working *everything* together for your good and ultimately His glory. You'll be able to rejoice in God's goodness, waiting expectantly for the day you'll see His face.

You'll be able to say to the Lord, "Even if I never get married, even if the guy I like never likes me back, even if my body isn't healed, even if my situation doesn't change, even if we always struggle financially, even if I can't understand why... EVEN IF! Oh Lord, *be glorified! Though I don't see You now, I will trust You and rejoice in You!*"

"Though you have not seen him, you love him. Though you do not now see him, you believe in him and rejoice with joy that is inexpressible and filled with glory" (1 Peter 1:8).

Footnotes

Chapter 2
1. Dr. John Irvine, *Laugh and Live Longer,* http://www.drjohnirvine.com/index.php?option=com_content&task=view&id=149&Itemid=27
2. Bower, B. "Look on the Bright Side and Survive Longer." *Science News,* May 26, 2001.

Chapter 3
1. White Horse Inn Ministry, www.whitehorseinn.org

Chapter 6
1. Strong's Concordance, Blue Letter Bible, www.blueletterbible.com
2. Strong's Lexicon, Blue Letter Bible, www.blueletterbible.com

Chapter 9
1. http://pages.prodigy.net/jhonig/bignum/qgalaxy.html
2. http://home.cwru.edu/~sjr16/advanced/

Chapter 12
1. C.H. Spurgeon, (1834-1892), *Sermon No. 222: The Christian's Heaviness and Rejoicing*; November 7, 1858

Chapter 15
1. C. H. Spurgeon, *Unbelievers Upbraided* June 8th, 1976

Printed in the United States
201277BV00024B/4-6/A